Cooperative QUILTS

CLASSROOM QUILTS FOR THE ENTIRE SCHOOL YEAR

By Diane Bonica and Kathy Devlin
Illustrations by Shelly Orchard

Fearon Teacher Aids
A Division of Frank Schaffer Publications, Inc.

To the patches of our lives that we love and cherish:
Adam, Andrew, Ashley, Jim, Jimmy, Joe, Matt, Michael,
Nancy, and Sarah.

A special thanks to the kindergarten students at
Charles F. Tigard and Discovery Elementary Schools.
Their handiwork provided the inspiration for this book.
D. B. , K. D., and S. O.

To Shaun, Alyssa, and Annie, all my love.
S. O.

Senior Editor: Kristin Eclov
Editor: Lisa Trumbauer
Cover and Inside Design: Rose Sheifer Graphic Productions
Inside Computer Illustration: Janet White
Cover Photography: Anthony Nex Photography

Fearon Teacher Aids
A Division of Frank Schaffer Publications, Inc.
23740 Hawthorne Boulevard
Torrance, CA 90505-5927

FE7947
ISBN 1-56417-947-8
3 4 5 6 7 8 9

Table of Contents

Introduction

Thematic learning is much like a puzzle. Several pieces fit tightly together to form a whole. What better way to emphasize this with students than by assembling a class quilt to celebrate their work? Creating class quilts serves many purposes: it is an exciting way to display students' work; it encourages children to work together, fostering cooperative learning; it can encompass many areas of the curriculum; and it enables you to share students' work with others. Simply fold the quilt as you would a blanket and transport it to another location. A quilt our kindergartners created first adorned our classroom wall. Now it is hanging at the city library!

Thematic learning ties many disciplines together. Each quilt project is designed to do the same as it incorporates science, math, social studies, reading, writing, and art. For example, the border of each quilt is a lesson in numbers, shapes, fractions, and colors. The main quilt pieces are children's artistic interpretations of the learning theme. The alternating squares are an art experience in texture, design, color, and form. Each quilt patch teaches. The entire quilt experience validates learning and exploring the theme.

Because we have made these quilts with our own classes, they have been designed with children's interests in mind as well as the practicality of the classroom. All quilts are created with materials readily available in school, namely butcher or mural paper, construction paper, and other art-project supplies. You might choose to use a quilt as a culminating event or even as the main part of a thematic unit. Either way, one thing is for certain—you and your students are celebrating the learning experience!

Quilts are a part of our national heritage. They proudly support our past and our quest to work together and share new ideas. Paper quilts add a new dimension to thematic study, adding a richness that comes from a cooperative project. With their colorful displays, quilts attract attention and say to kids, "We notice your work!" Cooperative quilts will hang in honor as symbols of group achievement.

How to Construct a Cooperative Quilt

Determining the Size of Your Quilt

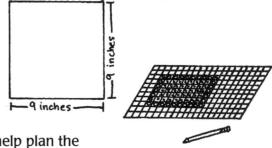

The quilt size will be based on the number of students in your class. For example, if you have 24 students, you will need 48 interior patches, two for each child. In addition, you will need 32 border patches. All patches are 9″ x 9″ (22.5 cm x 22.5 cm). A complete quilt for 24 students will measure 10 patches by 8 patches. To help plan the class quilt, first design and diagram the quilt on graph paper.

Step-by-Step Directions:

1. Roll out two 6-foot (180 cm) lengths of 36-inch (90 cm) butcher paper. Overlap the strips, and secure them with wide cellophane tape.

2. Instruct children to complete the quilt patches as described for each individual quilt.

3. Once children have completed their patches, arrange them on the butcher paper, starting with the border. Line up the border patches around the edge of the paper, beginning at the left corner. *Do not glue them down!*

4. Place the interior patches in an alternating pattern throughout the inside of the quilt. *Again, do not glue!*

5. Invite children to look at the quilt. Do they like it? Would they rearrange any of the patches? Encourage students to make suggestions about how to rearrange the blocks. This makes the quilt a completely cooperative effort.

6. Ask children to help glue each patch in place. (Hint: To secure the quilt, gently step on it while applying the patches.)

7. Invite children to vote on a catchy title for the quilt. Create a title sign or banner using a computer or gluing die-cut letters to butcher paper. Staple, tape, or glue the title above the quilt.

8. Display the quilt on a class wall or in the hallway for others to admire.

9. To store the quilt, fold it from top to bottom along the taped middle, then fold in half again. Finish by folding the quilt from side to side. Store the quilt in a plastic bag in a dry, dark area.

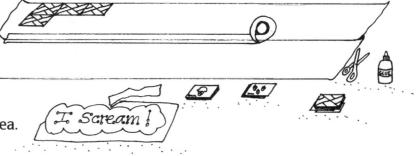

Additional Activity Directions

"Glyphs," the "Concentration" Game Board, the Feely Box, and the Peek Box are activities that can be used with all the quilts. The directions are provided below.

Glyph Key
Yellow rays— I've seen a rainbow
Orange rays— I've seen lightning
Gray rays— I've seen hail

What Is a Glyph?

For each quilt we have included a glyph factor. Glyphs are a way to collect, display, and interpret data. As students work on their quilt patches, ask them questions. Their answers determine how they will construct their quilt patches. For example, when constructing the weather quilt, ask children which weather phenomenon they have seen. To record their answers, each child creates a quilt patch using a particular paint color:

◆ Students who have seen a rainbow should paint the sun rays yellow.
◆ Students who have seen lightning should paint the sun rays orange.
◆ Students who have seen hail should paint the sun rays gray.

◆ Students who have seen more than one weather phenomenon should paint the sun rays with all the colors.

Place a color key near the quilt so viewers can obtain information about the students' weather experiences.

"Concentration" Game Board

Playing the game "Concentration" is an excellent way to hone children's memory and matching skills. Create a reusable "Concentration" game board. Start with a sheet of 22" x 28" (55 cm x 70 cm) oaktag or poster board. Write the game title at the top of the game board. Place 20 self-stick labels in five columns of four on the poster board. Laminate the entire board. For playing cards, cut 20 3" x 2" (7.5 cm x 5.0 cm) rectangles from poster board. Attach a blank sticker or label to each card. Draw 10 pairs of illustrated matching cards. The illustrations should relate to the quilt's theme. Laminate the playing cards to make them sturdy.

6

To play the game, place all cards face down on the game-board labels. Have children take turns flipping over two cards at a time to find a match. If a match is found, the player removes the cards from the game board and goes again. If not, it is the next player's turn. The game continues until all 10 matches have been found. The winner is the player with the most matched pairs.

Feely Box

Challenge children to test their tactile perceptions using a Feely Box. To make a Feely Box, use a sturdy cardboard box with a removable lid and an adult athletic sock. The box needs to be big enough to accommodate objects up to 10 inches (25 cm) in height and width. (Hint: Sugar ice-cream cone boxes work well.) Cut a 4-inch (10 cm) hole in the center of the lid, and cut off the toe of the sock. Stretch the top of the sock over the hole in the lid. Hot-glue or staple the sock securely in place. Pull the sock through the hole. Cover the outside of the box with colored adhesive paper.

Place an item inside the box. Ask students to reach in and identify the object by touch only. No peeking allowed!

Peek Box

Challenge children to identify objects by using a Peek Box. Cut a 4" x 1" (10 cm x 2.5 cm) slit in one end of a shoebox. Cut a 2" x 1" (5 cm x 2.5 cm) slit in the opposite end of the lid. Cover the box and lid with colored adhesive paper.

Secure a small item to the lid near the slit. Show children how to hold the box up to their eyes and peek through the large slit in the end of the box. Ask students if they can tell what item is inside. Record the children's responses on the chalkboard. Reveal the item in the box to check their guesses.

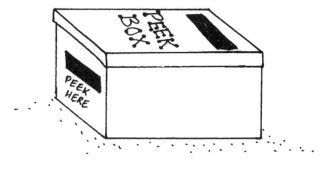

Bibliography

To learn more about quilts and quilt making, encourage children to read and enjoy these books.

Coerr, Eleanor. *The Josefina Story Quilt.* Harper Trophy, 1986.

de Paola, Tomie, and Tony Johnston. *The Quilt Story.* G.P. Putnam's Sons, 1985.

Ernst, Lisa Campbell. *Sam Johnson and the Blue Ribbon Quilt.* Lothrop, Lee and Shepard, 1983.

Flournoy, Valerie. *The Patchwork Quilt.* Dial Books, 1985.

Cole, Barbara Hancock. *Texas Star.* Orchard Books, 1990.

Hopkins, Judy. *Around the Block with Judy Hopkins.* That Patchwork Place, 1994.

Hopkinson, Deborah. *Sweet Clara and the Freedom Quilt.* Alfred A. Knopf, 1993.

Jonas, Ann. *The Quilt.* Greenwillow Books, 1984.

Martin, Jacqueline Briggs. *Bizzy Bones and the Lost Quilt.* Lothrop, Lee and Shepard, 1988.

Mills, Susan Winter. *Illustrated Index to Traditional American Quilt Patterns.* Arco Inc., 1980.

Morrison, Maighan. *Long Live Earth.* Scholastic, 1993.

Paul, Ann Whitford. *Eight Hands Round: A Patchwork Alphabet.* HarperCollins, 1991.

Polacco, Patricia. *The Keeping Quilt.* The Trumpet Club, 1988.

Apples Abound Quilt

It's as American as apple pie! And this apple quilt is sure to be just as pleasing. The simple square border boasts apple hues. The torn-paper trees add color and three-dimensional appeal. Sliced-apple prints finish the quilt with an early Americana design. Your students will enjoy learning and experimenting with this tasty American tradition.

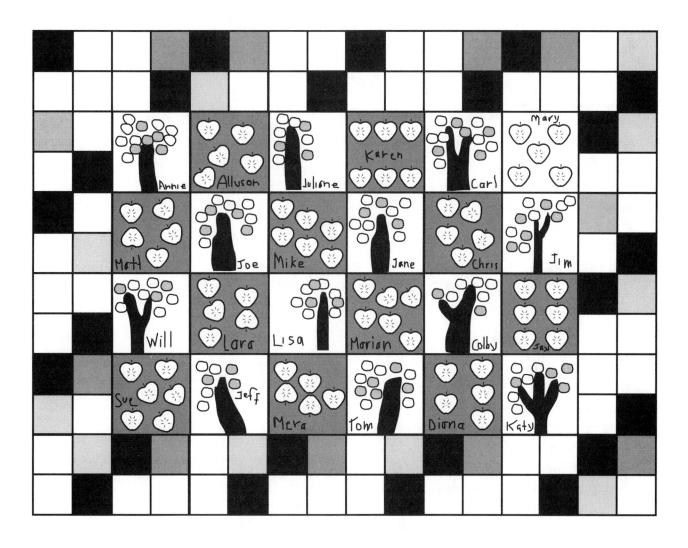

Border Patch

Invite children to help create the border for your apple quilt. Pass out red, green, white, and brown construction paper. Invite children to measure, then cut 4.5″ x 4.5″ (11.25 cm x 11.25 cm) construction-paper squares. Have each child arrange four squares into a quilt block and tape them together. Glue the quilt blocks around the edges of the butcher paper to make the border.

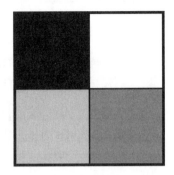

Apple Print Patch

Pass out yellow construction paper, and have students measure and cut out a 9″ x 9″ (22.5 cm x 22.5 cm) square. Set up a table with pans of paint in various colors. Cut apples in half vertically, and give one to each student. Show students how to dip the apple into the paint, then press it to the construction-paper square.

Glyph Factor

Directions for making glyphs are found on page 6. Ask the children how old they are and if they like apples. Have the children record their answers on their apple print patches.

- ◆ If students are 6 years old, make 6 apple prints.
- ◆ If students are 5 years old, make 5 apple prints.
- ◆ If students like apples, paint with red paint.
- ◆ If students don't like apples, paint with green paint.

Apple Tree Patch

Give each child a sheet of 9″ x 12″ (22.5 cm x 30 cm) light blue construction paper. Ask students to measure and cut out 9″ x 9″ (22.5 cm x 22.5 cm) squares. Invite children to tear and shape a brown tree trunk, red apples, and green leaves from scrap paper. Help children glue the tree parts together to make torn-paper apple trees. Glue the leaves to the tree trunk and the apples to the leaves. Once the apple trees are dry, glue them to the light blue square.

   1997 © Fearon Teacher Aids FE7947

Literature Connections

Book Activity

Share the book *Seasons of Arnold's Apple Tree,* by Gail Gibbons (Harcourt Brace, 1988), with the class. Pass out 6″ x 18″ (15 cm x 45 cm) strips of drawing paper. Challenge children to measure and then divide the strips into fourths. Invite them to draw a tree in each section of the paper strip to represent each season. Use crayons and markers to add details.

Pocket Chart

Copy the poem on oaktag or poster-board strips.

> *Apple pie, apple pie,*
> *I think I'll never see*
> *Anything as yummy*
> *As an apple pie for me.*

Replace the words, *apple pie* with *cherry pie, lemon pie, blueberry pie, pumpkin pie,* and so on, each time reciting the rhyme with the class. Talk with children about the different pies they like best.

Hanging Chart

Write the following poem on large chart paper. Teach it to the class, along with the body motions.

Way up high in the apple tree.	(Stretch up high)
Two little apples smiled at me.	(Wiggle fists in air)
I shook that tree as hard as I could	(Shake the trunk)
Down came the apples.	(Point down)
Mmmmm–they were good.	(Rub tummies)

Class Book: *"Apple Surprises"*

As children watch, cut an apple in half *horizontally* to reveal the star inside. Ask the class what they would like to find inside an apple. Pass out 9″ x 12″ (22.5 cm x 30 cm) red construction paper and the same-size drawing paper. Help each child cut out a large apple from the red paper. Show the children how to cut a door at the base of the apple. Glue the apple to the drawing paper, being careful *not* to glue down the door. Have them open the door and draw their surprises inside on the drawing paper. Invite each child to copy and complete the following sentence undeneath his or her apple:

"There is a _____ inside _____'s apple." Ask volunteers to create a book cover, then bind all the pages together with staples or yarn.

Journal Writing

Encourage children to describe how an apple tastes in their writing journals. Set up a tasting station of different kinds of apples for children to try. Invite them to complete this sentence in their journals: "My apple tastes _____ ."

Have children date the entries and add illustrations, too.

Celebrate Johnny Appleseed

Johnny Appleseed may be an American folk legend, but he also happens to be a real person. His real name was John Chapman, and he was born on September 26, 1774, in Massachusetts. No matter the time of year, have a Johnny Appleseed Day. As you greet the class, wear a pot on your head, as Johnny Appleseed did. Then share a book about Johnny Appleseed's life, such as *Johnny Appleseed,* by Steven Kellogg (Morrow, 1996). Serve apple slices for snacks.

   1997 © Fearon Teacher Aids FE7947

Math Activities

Counting Table

Draw 5 boxes on an 8.5" x 11" (21.3 cm x 27.5 cm) sheet of white paper. Then reproduce the paper and pass out it to the class. Have children write the following labels on the bottom of each box: *1 apple, 2 apples, 3 apples, 4 apples, more apples.* Encourage children to count and draw the correct number of apples in each box. Invite classmates to check each other's work.

Graphing

Ask children to bring in apples from home. Encourage them to select different varieties. On a long length of butcher paper, create 4 columns. Write these colors at the top of each column—red, yellow, green, and red/green. Have children place their apples under the appropriate color category. (To make the chart more sturdy, you might cover it with clear adhesive paper.) Have the children count and then compare each apple group. Ask the children which apple color had the most apples and the least apples.

Estimation

Hold up an apple and ask children to predict how many seeds are inside. Write children's predictions on the chalkboard. When all the guesses are in, cut open the apple and count the number of seeds. Discuss the children's predictions. Ask children if they think all apples have the same number of seeds. Show the children another kind of apple. Have them predict the number of seeds. Continue the activity as before by cutting open the apple. Compare the number of seeds in both apples. Help the children write greater than ($>$) or less than ($<$) equations comparing the number of seeds. For example, 8 seeds $>$ 6 seeds.

Weighing

Encourage children to use a balance scale to weigh and compare apples. Have students place an apple on one side of the scale, then place ceramic tiles or pennies into the other side until the scale balances. Instruct children to record their answers on a recording sheet with such sentences as: "My apple weighed 13 tiles." Challenge children to determine which apples weigh more by analyzing the numbers on their recording sheets.

"Concentration" Game

Make "Concentration" cards (see directions on page 6) using 10 different pairs of matching apple pictures. Place the cards in random order on the game board. Encourage children to take turns matching the pair of apple pictures. The child with the most matches at the end of the game wins.

Problem Solving

Incorporate apples into math word problems. For example: Ten apples hung from a tree. You picked 3. How many apples are left? Encourage children to come up with and illustrate their own math problems. Invite them to share their math problems with a partner. If interested, make apple cutouts for math manipulatives.

"Guess the Category" Game

Gather 12 items from around the classroom for children to sort. Six items need to be red. Conceal them in a bag. Arrange two large plastic hoops or circles of yarn on the floor. Place a card with the word "Yes" in one circle, and the word "No" in the other. Remove a red item from the bag, and place it in the "yes" circle. Continue removing items one at a time from the bag. Challenge children to decide in which circle each item belongs. Once all the items have been sorted, ask the children what all the items in the "yes" circle have in common. Confirm that they are all red.

Patterning

Challenge children to recognize and create patterns using real apples of different colors or apple shapes cut from red, green, and yellow construction paper or flannel. Arrange the apples in a recognizable pattern. Ask the children to "read" it with you starting from left to right. (Left-to-right orientation builds reading-readiness skills.) For example, one pattern might "read" red, green, red, green. Have children come up with the next apple in the pattern. Encourage children to create their own apple patterns for classmates to "read."

 1997 © Fearon Teacher Aids FE7947

Science Activities

Experimentation

Most children are probably familiar with how ordinary apples taste. But do they know how dried apples taste? Bring in a fruit or apple dehydrator. (If a dehydrator is not available, dried apple slices may be available in a local grocery or health food store.) Invite children to help slice apples with plastic knives. Place the slices in the dehydrator and watch them change. Pass out the dried apple slices for children to taste and compare. Have the children write sentences in their writing journals, comparing the taste, appearance, and texture of dried apples and fresh apples.

Classification

If possible, use the apples children brought in for the graphing activity on page 13. Encourage children to classify the apples in several ways. For example:

◆ Apples with or without stems

◆ Large, medium, or small apples

◆ Apples with or without bruises

◆ Apples bought in stores or picked in backyards

Invite children to come up with their own apple categories.

Observation

Cut two different sizes of apples in half horizontally. Have children draw the star shape inside the apple. Compare the sizes of the stars and the number of seeds found inside each apple. Ask them if the size of the apple makes a difference to the star shape or the number of seeds. Invite the children to add the drawings and their observations to their science journals.

Cooking

Here's a simple applesauce recipe to try. Cut about four cored apples into chunks, and place them in a blender. Add about a ¼ cup (60 ml) of water and set the blender to grind. Add sugar or cinnamon to taste. Spoon the applesauce into cups for children to enjoy. Make as much applesauce as needed for each child to have a sample.

Investigation and Observation

If the time of year and climate are right, arrange a class field trip to a local apple orchard. Many orchards provide educational tours for school children. As a class, make a list of things they would like to learn about apples and how they grow. Pose the questions to your apple-orchard guide. Children will probably learn that in order for apples to grow, bees are needed to cross-pollinate apple blossoms. Once pollen from one flower gets inside another flower, an apple starts to grow. Often, orchards will allow children to pick a few apples to take home, as well as press apples into cider for children to taste. Make sure that children wash their apples before eating them. After returning to class, have children dictate a class thank-you note to the orchard and their guide.

Tactile Table

Set up a Tactile Table for children to learn through touch experiences. Gather some apple-related products for children to feel, such as apple stems, cores, seeds, and peels. Encourage children to describe the different textures they feel and to write the words in their science or writing journals.

1997 © Fearon Teacher Aids FE7947

Art Activities

Easel Painting

Draw and cut out a large tree trunk and branches from brown mural paper, and tape it to a wall. Explain that the students are going to make an apple tree. Provide paints, paper, and easels, and real apples for children to use as models. Make sure children wear protective smocks. Encourage the students to paint the apples they see. Once the painted apples have dried, help the children cut them out and tape them to the tree branches. Ask the students if there is something missing from the apple tree. Give each child a sheet of green construction paper to make leaves. Then tape them to the branches.

Apple-Head People

Invite children to paint apple-head people. Give each child a sheet of painting paper. First, paint a large apple shape at the top of the paper. Allow the apple to dry, then paint the face. When the paint is dry, draw a body below the apple head. Invite children to name their apple people, and take their paintings home to share with their families. Invite the students to write a class story about the apple-head people.

Computer Apple Art

If a computer drawing program is available to your class, invite children to use it to draw apples. Have the students print out their computer apples. Encourage them to compare their computer drawings with their painted apples. Ask the students which apples they like better, the computer drawn ones or the painted ones. Display the computer apple art in your computer center.

Names and Faces Quilt

As children learn about each other, they realize that not only do they have things in common, but differences that make them unique and special. The Names and Faces quilt is the perfect way to start the school year or to welcome new students to your class. The patches encourage students to draw self-portraits and colorful name designs. And the border patches combine simple shapes for children to create homes. Display the quilt for children to learn about and appreciate each other.

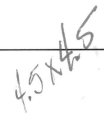

4.5 x 4.5

Border Patch

Invite children to create a border of homes that integrates primary colors and basic shapes. Give each student a 9" x 9" (22.5 cm x 22.5 cm) square of yellow construction paper for the background and blue and red construction paper scraps for making their homes. Have children cut square houses, rectangular apartment buildings, town homes from red paper, and triangular roof pieces from blue. Glue the shapes to the yellow patch. Encourage the children to use paper scraps to add round yellow windows and rectangular or square doors.

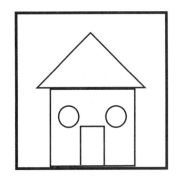

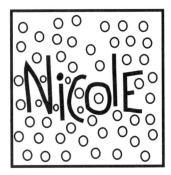

Name Patch

Set up an art table with white 9" x 9" (22.5 cm x 22.5 cm) squares, sponge-tipped bottles of red, yellow, and blue paint, glue, and a pie plate of gold glitter. Show children how to dot the white patch with the paint. When the paint has dried, have each child write his or her name in glue, then dip the patch in gold glitter.

Glyph Factor

Directions for making glyphs are found on page 6. Encourage children to share how they received their names. Have them record their answers on their name patches.
- ◆ If a student was named after someone in his or her family, use blue paint to write the name.
- ◆ If a student's parents chose the name because they liked it, use red paint to write his or her name.
- ◆ If a student's parents chose the name for other reasons, use yellow paint to write his or her name.

Self-Portrait Patch

Provide students with yarn in many colors, fabric scraps, construction paper in various skin tones, crayons, and glue. Invite children to use the materials to create self-portraits. Glue the portraits to blue 9" x 9" (22.5 cm x 22.5 cm) construction-paper patches.

Literature Connections

Book Activity

As a class, read a book about names, such as *A, My Name Is Alice,* by Steven Kellogg (Puffin, 1995). As you share the book a second time, encourage children to replace the names in the story with classmates' names or names of family members. Tape record retelling the story. Play the tape for the class and have children point to their classmates' portraits on the quilt.

Pocket Chart

Copy the poem below on oaktag or poster-board strips. Make sure you have one strip for each letter of the alphabet. Be sure to include each child's name with the appropriate letter. Substitute letters and names as you read each verse.

Let's play a game,
To learn a new name.
A name that starts with A,
Alyssa, Adam, Arman start with A.

Create a bar graph to record the first letters of students' names. Ask them to look at the graph and identify which letters have the most names and the least names.

Hanging Chart

To help with letter recognition, review the traditional "ABC" song with the class. Write the alphabet and the words of the song on a hanging chart. Point to each letter as children sing it. Point to each letter again, and have children whose names start with that letter raise their hands. Have children say their names and accent the beginning sounds.

"All About Me" Bags

As a homework assignment, invite children to fill a quart-size (.95 l) self-sealing plastic bag with five items that tell about them. For example, they might include a family photo, a favorite toy, a souvenir from a trip, pictures of favorite foods cut from magazines, and so on. Each day, allow time for several children to share their items. Display the bags in a "class museum," with labels indicating whom the objects belong to. After everyone has shared, have children take their items home again.

Class Photo Album

Over several days, take pictures of your class involved in various activities. Try to capture groups of three or more children, making sure everyone has been photographed. Explain that you are making a class photo album. Glue the photos to heavy paper, then ask children to help write captions for each one. Sentences should be simple and similar so children can read them on their own. For example, "Ruben, Sarah, and Mike are painting." "Nicole, Najwa, and Ashleigh are building." Ask volunteers to create a cover for the album. Bind all the pages together with yarn. Invite children to enjoy the book together.

Class Name Book

Create a class alphabet book of names featuring the children in class. Arrange children into groups according to the first letters of their names. Help them write a sentence on the page, such as, "B is for Blake, Brandon, and Bobbi." Then ask students to draw pictures of themselves. Invite one child each day to take the book home to show his or her family.

A is for Annie, Amy, and Alena.

C is for Christine and Cathy.

B is for Blake, Brandon, and Bobbi.

Sing a Song of Names

Celebrate children's names by singing this simple name song, sung to the tune of, "Row, Row, Row Your Boat."

Christine, Christine, Christine's my name.
Sing it if you please!
Christine, Christine, Christine, Christine
That's the name for me!

If possible, you might obtain a recording of the song "Willoughby Wallaby Woo" by Raffi (*The Raffi Singable Songs Collection*, A & M Records, 1988). Share it with the class, then invite them to sing the song, substituting their own names to hear the silly changes. Be sure to include your own name, too!

Printing Center

Set up a table with alphabet stamps. Have children use the stamps to print their own names. Encourage children to visit the center in groups, printing group members' names as well.

Math Activities

Counting and Graphing

Create a bar graph to record the number of letters in the students' names. Have each child write his or her name on paper, then count the letters and write the number. Write the numbers from 1 to 10 down the left side of the chart. Have each child identify the number of letters in his or her name. Draw a smiley face next to the number of letters in the child's name. Help children interpret the chart. Ask the students which numbers have the most smiley faces and the least smiley faces. Discuss what information they can get from the chart.

1	
2	☺ ☺
3	☺ ☺ ☺ ☺
4	☺ ☺ ☺ ☺ ☺ ☺ ☺ ☺ ☺ ☺ ☺ ☺
5	☺ ☺ ☺ ☺ ☺ ☺ ☺
6	☺ ☺
7	☺
8	☺
9	
10	

Estimation

Fill a jar with an assortment of plastic alphabet letters. Challenge children to estimate how many letters are in the jar. Write the children's estimates on the chalkboard. Invite two children to count the letters to determine the correct amount. Encourage small groups to experiment with the letters to see how many names they can spell.

"Guess the Category" Game

Write children's names on index cards. Sort the names into different categories, such as names with the same beginning sound, names that have four letters, names of children who sit in a particular row, and so on. Create two circles on a bulletin board, and write "Yes" in one circle and "No" in the other. Select cards and invite children to help read them. Tape each card in the appropriate circle. Encourage children to guess the category. For example, the names Sam, Shurae, Shannon, and Steve would be in the "yes" circle, and the names Edgar, Ashton, and Mei would be in the "no" circle.

"Concentration" Game

Suggest that children play a game of "Concentration" using the names of classmates as playing cards. Invite each child to create two similar name cards for him- or herself. Then set up the game as directed in the instructions on page 6.

Measuring

Have students spell their names using plastic alphabet letters. Help children use rulers to measure the length of their names. Invite them to write the measurements in inches (or centimeters). Help them compare and contrast their results. Whose name is longest? Shortest? How can they tell?

Problem Solving

For simple addition problems, have children write their full names, including first, middle, and last names. Have them count the number of letters in each name, and write the number below it. Challenge the children to add all the letters together to find the total number of letters in the class.

Science Activities

Research

Encourage children to investigate homes around the world. Provide children with non-fiction books about particular world regions, such as Asia, Africa, Europe, South and Central America. Have students identify the different types of homes they see around the world. Invite children to draw pictures of different kinds of homes and include brief explanations of where the homes are found.

Observing Animal Habitats

Talk with children about where animals live. Come up with a list of ideas, for example, birds live in nests, spiders live in webs, bees live in hives, ants live in holes and tunnels, and fish live in water. If possible, locate a habitat for children to observe firsthand. Look for an active bird's nest or spider web to observe but be careful not to disturb it. You might set up an ant farm, reptile terrarium, or fish aquarium. Discuss with children why these homes are perfect for the animals that live there.

Texture Table

To help children with letter recognition, invite them to explore letters through tactile experiences. Collect an assortment of letters, such as macaroni, plastic, cookie-cutter, and foam letters. Challenge children to close their eyes, select a letter, and identify it by touch.

Cooking

When we cook foods, we alter or change them in some way. This is true even when toasting bread! Bring a toaster, paper plates, loaves of bread, plastic knives, butter or jelly, and food coloring to school. Give each student a slice of bread and a cotton swab. Invite them to print their names using food coloring and cotton swabs. Ask students what they think will happen if the bread is toasted. How will the color and texture change? Toast children's slices to find out. Invite them to enjoy their toast with butter or jelly.

Classification

Have nature magazines on hand for children to cut up. Invite groups to cut out pictures of animals they find interesting. Combine all the pictures together. Challenge children to classify the pictures in various ways, for example, big, medium, and small animals; animals that live in deserts, cold areas, or forests; animals that have hooves versus animals with paws; or by groups, such as birds, reptiles, and mammals.

Science Journal

Take the class for a nature walk to observe an animal in its natural habitat. For example, children might see a squirrel foraging for acorns, or ants carrying bread crumbs, or butterflies sipping flower nectar. Even if you live in a city, some of these animals might be easy to spot, or invite children to observe an animal in a class habitat. Encourage students to write a sentence or two in their science journals about the animal, such as, "I saw an ant digging a tunnel," or "I saw a fish eating fish food." Suggest that they include an illustration with their entries.

Class Visitor—Communication Companies

Names are very important to communication companies, such as telephone companies, internet providers, and so on. Most households are assigned at least one telephone number. Invite a representative from a local telephone company or internet provider to visit your class to talk about the importance of names and numbers and how they are used to communicate all over the world. Many communication companies may already have programs for children.

Art Activities

Magazine People Art

Pass out magazines and invite children to cut out faces from articles and advertisements. Have them glue the faces to construction paper. Challenge each child to paint or draw the body of his or her magazine person doing an activity. Encourage them to name their magazine people and display their work around the room.

Paper Doll Family Activity

Send an oaktag paper doll and a note home with each student. The note should invite family members to help their child create a paper doll of himself or herself. Encourage them to be as creative as they wish. Suggest that the children make three-dimensional dolls using yarn for hair and fabric scraps for clothes. Invite children to share their self-portrait paper dolls with the class.

Computer Name Art

If a computer is available, invite children to print out their names using different computer fonts, styles, sizes, and colors. Encourage the children to experiment until they come up with a name design they like. Have children print their fancy names, then use them as plaques to identify and decorate their desks.

Spider Surprises

Capture the eight-legged excitement of spiders with this dramatic quilt. Encourage children to create webs through marble painting, as well as to make pop-up, big-eyed spiders. Large triangular border patches add depth and an intriguing design to the spider quilt. The study of arachnids is sure to wiggle its way into students' imaginations.

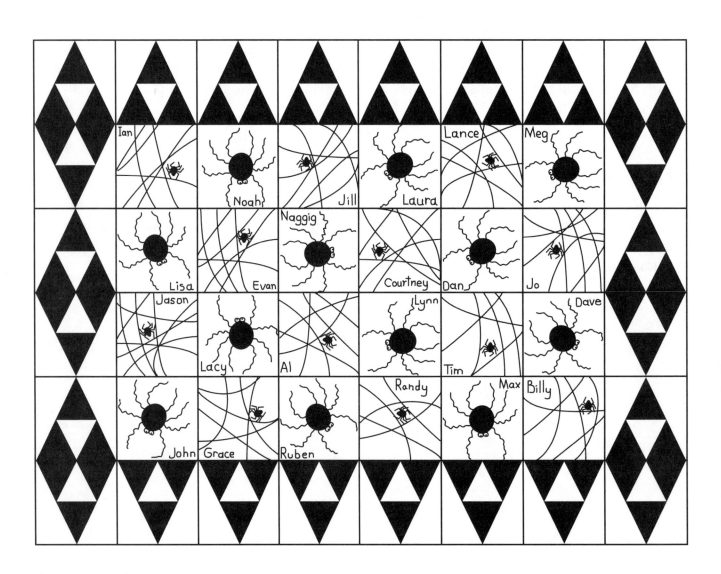

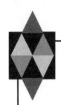
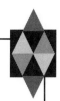

Border Patch

First draw the triangular pattern of the border patch on the chalkboard. Then pass out a 9" x 9" (22.5 cm x 22.5 cm) square of white construction paper to each student. Help children draw the triangular design using rulers and pencils. Color in three triangles with black marker as shown, or cut triangles from black construction paper to glue in place.

Spider Patch

Give each student a yellow 9"x 9" (22.5 cm x 22.5 cm) square of construction paper. Help children cut a circle with a diameter of about 6 inches (15 cm) from black construction paper to fit in the center. Have them cut eight black construction-paper strips. Show the children how to accordion-fold the strips for spider legs. Have children glue the legs to the circle. To complete their spiders, pass out dot stickers for children to create eyes. Make sure children write their names on their spider patches.

Glyph Factor

Directions for making glyphs are found on page 6. Ask the children how they would react to a spider. Have the children record their answers using different colored eyes on their spider patches.

- ◆ If they would hold a spider, use green dot stickers for spider eyes.
- ◆ If they would not hold a spider, use orange dot stickers for spider eyes.
- ◆ If they would run away from a spider, use yellow dot stickers for spider eyes.

Web Patch

Invite children to marble paint a 9" x 9" (22.5 cm x 22.5 cm) white quilt patch for a spider-web design. Have each child place a white square in a large shoebox lid. Show them how to dip a marble in black paint, then place it on the patch. Help children to tilt the box lid so the marble rolls along the patch, leaving behind a black wavy line. When the patch has dried, suggest that students glue a plastic or paper spider to the web. Have children write their names on the patch, too.

Literature Connections

Book Activity

As a class, read the book *One Hungry Spider,* by Jeannie Baker (E P Dutton, 1982). Help the children imagine what it might be like to be a spider. What would they catch in their webs? Encourage children to draw spider webs on art paper. Invite children to flip though magazines to find pictures of the things they would catch in their spider webs. Have them cut them out, then glue the pictures to their webs.

Pocket Chart

Challenge children to come up with a variety of words to describe how a spider moves, such as dance, crawl, climb, jump, creep, spin, and hang. List their words on the chalkboard or on chart paper. Copy the poem below on sentence strips. Have children recite the rhyme, and each time, replace the underlined word with one from the list.

Spin spider spin,
On your web for me.
Spin spider spin,
For everyone to see.

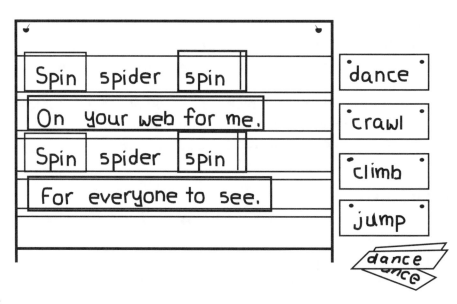

Hanging Poem Chart

If children aren't already familiar with it, teach them the rhyme "Eensie Weensie Spider." Write it on a hanging chart. Point to each word as you recite it with the children. For added excitement, attach a plastic spider to fishing line. Dangle the line over your hanging chart, then, as children recite the poem, pull it up to watch the spider creep up the paper. Lower the line to replicate the spider being washed away by the rain.

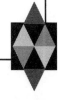

Class Spider Book

Share with children the book *The Very Busy Spider,* by Eric Carle (Putnam, 1989). Create a class book about what might happen if a busy spider came to visit your class. Jot down sentences similar to those in the book. Invite children to illustrate their pages, then read the story back to the class.

Writing Journal and Feely Box

How do children really feel about spiders? Encourage them to write their feelings in their writing journals. Provide them with a sentence starter, such as, "I think spiders are _____ ." To further prompt their writing, place a toy spider in the Feely Box (see directions on page 7). As children feel the spider, ask them to pay attention to their reactions, then write about them in their journals.

Webs for Family and Friends

Supply students with glitter pens and dark-colored construction paper. Invite them to draw a web and write a message to a friend or family member. Have children write the message as if the spider spun it inside the web, or provide markers for children to write their messages below the web.

Math Activities

Graphing

Not all spider webs look alike. The round webs children are most familiar with are called *orb webs.* But children might also have seen cobwebs, like those found in basements. Sheet webs are also common. They are usually seen within the branches of bushes or blades of grass. Some webs look like triangles, others like funnels, and still others like bowls. Ask children what kinds of webs they have seen. Choose three to four webs common to your area and draw each at the top of a chart column. Have children write their names on stickers to place in the columns of the webs they have seen. Which kind of web is the most common? Which seems to be the most rare? How can children tell?

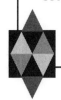

Estimation

Ask children to actually look for spider webs in and around school. Invite children to estimate the number of webs they will find, then take a walk around the school to investigate. Record each web children see and its location. If your spider-web count is surprisingly low, explain that an entire school of children might frighten spiders away. Spiders usually spin their webs in an area that is relatively quiet so the web won't be disturbed.

Spider Counting Game

Divide a 9" x 12" (22.5 cm x 30 cm) poster board or sheet of construction paper into 20 squares. Then laminate the game board. Provide 20 plastic spiders (or have children draw them on squares of paper) and a game die. Invite children to take turns rolling the die, counting out spiders, and placing the amount on the game board, one in each square. Have children write addition problems using the spiders. For example, 6 spiders + 1 spider = 7 spiders. Children can also work on simple subtraction problems as well. For example, 25 spiders − 4 spiders = 1 spider.

Spider Dominoes

Invite children to play a game of "Spider Dominoes." Ahead of time, create 30 domino playing pieces. Cut poster board into 3" x 6" (7.5 cm x 15 cm) strips. Divide the strips in half, and draw a spider in each half. Draw different amounts of dots on the spiders' bodies for children to count and match. Be sure to leave some halves blank as well.

Problem Solving

Invite children to count spider legs to solve math problems. Pose such a problem as, "If you have two spiders, how many legs are there in all?" Encourage children to draw the spiders, making sure each has eight legs. Then have children count all the legs to solve the problem.

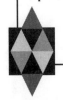

Sorting

Many other things have legs beside people, animals, insects, and spiders, such as tables, chairs, desks, and other furniture. Provide children with magazines. Have them cut out all the things they see with legs. Challenge students to sort the items by how many legs each has.

Measuring

Divide the class into groups to measure items. Give each group 36 one-inch (2.5 cm) squares. Have the children draw a spider on the square. Use the spider squares to measure different items in the classroom. Have the children estimate the length of an item and then measure it to check their estimations. For example, children could measure their desk tops, chair seats, a chalkboard ledge, a bookshelf, a book, and a ruler, to name a few. Set up a chart for children to record their ideas, drawing pictures of the objects they measured, then writing how many spiders it was in length.

Science Activities

Modeling a Spider Web

Invite students to create a large spider web on the classroom floor. Seat the class in a circle, and hand out three balls of yarn. Have children tape the yarn to the floor, then roll the ball to a child sitting across the circle. Ask the new child to tape the yarn again, and roll the ball to another student. The web is complete when the floor resembles a spider's habitat. Encourage children to pretend they are spiders as they walk in the spaces of the web.

Observing Spiders

Take the children on a nature walk to look for spider webs to observe, or locate one you recorded earlier during your estimation activity. Invite children to bring along their science journals. As children watch the web, caution them to be quiet so they won't spook the spider. Visit the same web on various days to notice any changes. Have children draw the spider in its web and any insects the spider has caught.

Spider Web Collection

If your class has observed a spider web that appears to be vacant, collect it for children to look at more closely. Or, capture a spider web from around your home to share with children. To save a spider web, spray it with hairspray, then place a piece of dark paper behind it, and move the paper to the web until the web sticks. Invite interested children to lightly feel the web and study its construction, adding their impressions to their science journals.

Cooking

Invite children to make spider cookies! Give each child a chocolate sandwich cookie, black licorice rope, and two golden raisins. Show children how to break up the licorice into eight pieces and to stick each section into the filling of the cookie. Have children complete their spider cookies by placing the raisins on top for eyes. Eat and enjoy!

Classification

Spiders generally fall into two categories—web weavers and hunters. Web weavers are generally slim and smallish, like garden spiders, black widows, and basic house spiders. Hunter spiders are of the larger, hairy variety, such as tarantulas, trap-door spiders, and wolf spiders. Invite children to flip through nonfiction science books to see the different kinds of spiders. Have them classify the spiders they see as web weavers or hunters. Invite the children to draw their spiders on a comparison chart.

Tactile Table

Purchase from a local hobby or craft shop a number of spider-related products, such as web material, plastic spiders, and even fake flies. Arrange the materials in a box or on a table, and invite children to visit for a tactile spider sensation.

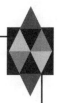

Class Visitor—Spider Expert

Check with a children's museum or zoo for a resident spider expert. Invite the spider expert to visit the class, perhaps bringing in several spiders for children to see firsthand. Encourage children to ask the expert any questions they have about spiders. Make sure the class sends a thank-you note after the visit.

Art Activities

Spider Headbands

Invite children to make creepy spider headbands. Help each student measure a strip of black construction paper to fit around his or her head, then staple the ends securely. Cut eight 12" x 1" (30 cm x 2.5 cm) strips of black construction paper for legs. Show the children how to accordion-fold the legs and staple them to the headband. Have children draw eyes on the front of their headbands. Invite children to wear their headbands as they complete activities or listen to spider stories.

Easel Painting

Encourage children to paint a portrait of an anatomically correct spider. A spider has two body parts—the cephalothorax (combined head and thorax) and the abdomen. Its eight legs and two-to-eight eyes should both be drawn on the cephalothorax only. When dry, display the spider paintings on a spider-web bulletin board.

Dramatic Play

Create a spider puppet using a black sock with eight black chenille stems stapled to it. Glue on plastic-foam balls for eyes. Encourage children to use the puppet to act out spider stories and songs they know. Play the song "Spider on the Floor" by Raffi (*The Raffi Singable Songs Collection*, A & M Records, 1988). Choose one child to move the spider puppet to different parts of his or her body as the class sings the song. Select a new child for each verse.

Scarecrow Sightings Quilt

No crows will fly away from your class when they make this attractive and inviting harvest quilt! Patches of pumpkins fill the border squares. Crows inspired by children's illustrator Ed Emberley boldly stand next to patches of friendly men of straw. Students will laugh as they piece together this autumn scene. It's the perfect way to welcome the fall season.

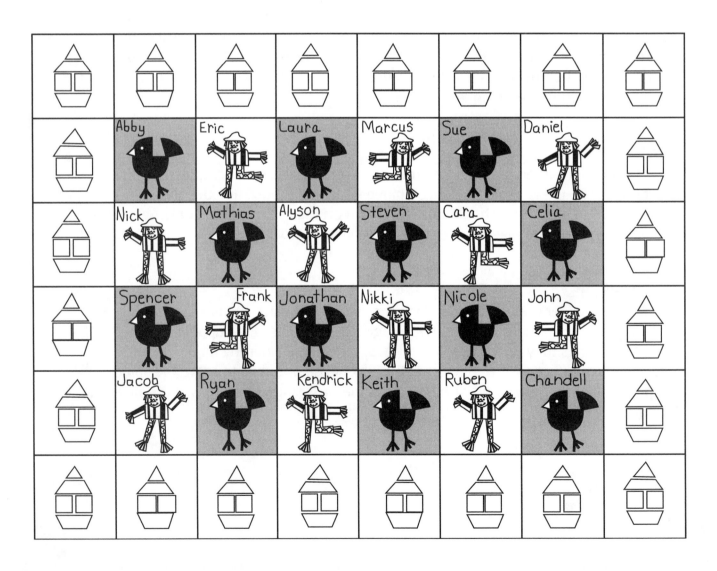

Border Patch

To create the border patch, give each student a 9" x 9" (22.5 cm x 22.5 cm) square of yellow construction paper. Have them cut out two trapezoids, two squares from orange construction paper, and a triangle from green construction paper. Help each child arrange the pieces to form a pumpkin. Glue the pieces in place to the yellow square.

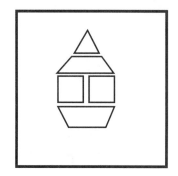

Scarecrow Patch

Set up a table with fabric scraps. Show children how to cut the following shapes from the fabric pieces—four thin rectangles for arms and legs, one thicker rectangle for the body, one square for the head, and one hat shape. Have children glue the pieces to a 9" x 9" (22.5 cm x 22.5 cm) orange square. For an added touch, invite children to glue crinkled yellow paper scraps to the ends of arms and legs to look like straw.

Glyph Factor

Directions for making glyphs are found on page 6. Ask the children what kinds of faces would they carve on their jack-o'-lanterns. Have the children record their answers on their scarecrow patches.

- ◆ If children would carve pumpkins with scary faces, glue the scarecrows' arms pointing straight out.
- ◆ If children would carve pumpkins with funny faces, glue the scarecrows' arms pointing upward.
- ◆ If children would carve pumpkins with happy faces, glue the scarecrows' arms pointing downward.

Crow Patch

The crow patches have been inspired by illustrations in Ed Emberly's book *Picture Pie* (Little, Brown, 1993). Share the book with children ahead of time. For the crow patch, start by passing out 9" x 9" (22.5 cm x 22.5 cm) squares of green construction paper, as well as black 5-inch (12.5 cm) diameter construction-paper circles. Have students fold the circles in half, then in half again. Cut the circle in half along one of the folded lines. Glue one half circle to the green square (see illustration). Cut the other half circle in half again. Show children how to arrange the quarter pieces for the tail and head. Have children add an orange paper beak and draw on crow's feet.

Literature Connections

Book Activity

Share the book *The Little Old Lady Who Was Not Afraid of Anything,* by Linda Williams (HarperCollins, 1986). As you read, invite children to come up with hand and body motions for each part of the scarecrow. Invite children to retell the story on a flannelboard.

Pocket Chart

The following rhyme is wonderful for oral reading. Write the lines on sentence strips to place in a pocket chart. Run your finger along each word, pausing before the rhyming words for children to sound them out.

Pumpkins by the wagon.   *Pumpkins by the hat.*
Pumpkins by the door.   *Pumpkins by the house.*
Pumpkins by the table.   *Pumpkins by the tree.*
Pumpkins by the floor.   *Pumpkins by the mound.*
Pumpkins by the scarecrow.   *Pumpkins by the gate.*
Pumpkins by the mouse.   *Pumpkins all around.*

Challenge students to come up with their own rhymes. Ask them where they might stack or leave a pumpkin. Write the children's verses on new sentence strips. Encourage them to illustrate each line.

Hanging Poem Chart

Write the following poem on a hanging chart or on poster paper. Invite the class to join in choral reading the poem. Encourage them to come up with hand motions, too.

There was a funny man,
With straw in his head.
When he scared the crows,
This is what he said:
"Go away!
Go away!
Go away, crow!
Let my pumpkins grow and grow."

Scarecrow Song

Teach children this scarecrow song, sung to the tune of "Skip to My Lou." Ask them what else might the scarecrow do to scare crows away. Invite the children to substitute the word *hop* with such words as *skip, clap, wave,* and *nod.*

Funny scarecrow, hop for us!
Funny scarecrow, hop for us!
Funny scarecrow, hop for us!
Scare the crows away.

Class Scarecrow Book

Ask the children if they were scarecrows, what they would do to keep the crows from eating the farmer's corn. Create a class book of the children's ideas. Give each child a sheet of paper. Have them complete the sentence, "If _____ were a scarecrow, he or she would _____ ." For example, "If Matt were a scarecrow, he would feed the crows corncobs." Have children write their sentences and then illustrate them. Bind all the pages together and have volunteers make a book cover.

Writing Journal

Place a miniature pumpkin in your Feely Box. (see directions on page 7). Invite children to feel the object, but don't tell them what it is. Have children write about the object in their writing journals. Ask the children to identify the item. Reveal the small pumpkin and brainstorm with children words to describe the way it looks and feels.

Pumpkin Writing Table

Set up a writing table with pumpkin patterns, or pumpkin stamps, and ink pads. Invite children to create pumpkin writing paper. Trace the pumpkins or use stamps to decorate the paper. Encourage children to write a few sentences about their own experiences with pumpkins or a very short pumpkin story.

Math Activities

Graphing

Cut scarecrow shirts from wrapping paper with two different patterns. Draw two columns on a sheet of chart paper. Glue one shirt above each column. Present the chart and shirt patterns to the class. Ask the children which shirt they like best. Have children sign their names under the preferred shirt. Which shirt is the class favorite? How can children tell? Have students count the names in each column and write the numbers on the chalkboard to identify the class choice.

Which scarecrow shirt do you like best?	
Tyler Matt Rachel Nicole Laura	Natalie Luke Spencer Sue Raul Jake

Estimation

Bring a medium-sized pumpkin to class with the top already removed (so you don't need to bring a knife to class). Explain that there are seeds inside the pumpkin. Ask the children to estimate the number of seeds in the pumpkin. Write children's estimations on the chalkboard. Invite each child to reach in and grab a handful of the pulpy, seed-filled insides. Dump the filling into a bowl. Have children help count the seeds. Pumpkins often have dozens of seeds. To aid in counting, suggest that children count in groups of ten. Which estimated number is closest to the actual amount?

Measuring

Invite children to create a life-sized stuffed scarecrow to use for measuring and comparing activities. Bring in old pants, a shirt, gloves, socks, a hat, and a pillowcase for the head. Divide the class into small groups. Show each group how to stuff a body part with newspapers. Line up the scarecrow body pieces on the floor for the children to measure. Invite children to use tape measures to compare the scarecrows' body measurements to the children's own body measurements. For example, the scarecrows' head is 24 inches (60 cm) around. Sarah's head is 18 inches (45 cm) around.

Weighing

Bring in pumpkins of various sizes for children to weigh and compare. (If appropriate, invite each child to bring in a pumpkin from home.) Suggest that children "weigh" a pumpkin in each hand for comparison. Ask children which they think weighs more or less. Have them check their predictions by using a balance scale or a regular scale to weigh their pumpkins.

"Guess the Category" Game

Collect six items that traditionally represent fall, such as a pumpkin, a football, a brown leaf, a school book, an acorn, and a Pilgrim hat. Then collect six items that represent spring or summer, such as sandals, a beach ball, a flower, a green leaf, and a bathing suit. Gather all the items in a brown grocery bag so children can't see them. Create two circles on the floor using either yarn or chalk. Place a sign in one circle that reads "Yes" and a sign in the other that reads "No." Pull a fall item from the bag, and place it in the "yes" circle. Challenge children to guess how the items are being sorted.

Patterning

Create jack-o'-lantern faces for children to make patterns. Draw three to four different faces on separate sheets of paper. Make four copies of each sheet. Divide the class into small groups. Present the groups with the jack-o'-lantern pictures. Encourage them to come up with patterns for classmates to figure out and continue, such as AABAA or ABCABC.

Science Activities

Science Journal

Divide the class into small groups. Give each group a section of pumpkin on a paper plate and a plastic knife. Encourage children to cut the pumpkin sections horizontally, vertically, and diagonally. Invite children to draw the different pumpkin views in their science journals.

Cooking

Pumpkin seeds make wonderful, healthy snacks! If children counted pumpkin seeds earlier, rinse the seeds with water and dry them with paper towels. Place the seeds on a cookie sheet, and roast them in an oven at 250°F for about an hour. Sprinkle the seeds with salt, and pass out cupfuls for children to try.

Experiment

What does a young pumpkin plant look like? Divide the class into small groups. Give each group a milk carton with soil and a few pumpkin seeds. Have the children plant the pumpkin seeds. Make sure they keep the soil moist, but not flooded, and that the cartons are exposed to sunlight. (For extra experimentation, you might predict what will happen to plants that receive less light, keeping those cartons in a darker area of the room.) Encourage children to draw the progress of their growing pumpkin plants in their science journals. If space and time allow, you might replant the pumpkins outdoors. Children will notice a vine begin to grow, along with a yellow flower. Once cross-pollinated by bees, a pumpkin will start to grow at the flower's base. Be aware that pumpkins need a lot of room to grow!

Tactile Table

Place straw and pumpkins on the tactile table for children to explore using their senses of touch. Encourage them to write their impressions in their science or writing journals.

Investigation

If the season and climate is right, locate a local pumpkin grower for children to visit. As a class, record any questions the children would like to ask the farmer about pumpkins. Make sure children notice how pumpkins grow along a vine on the ground and that ripe pumpkins are usually bright orange. If possible, invite children to pick a pumpkin to take home. After returning to the classroom have children dictate a thank-you letter to send to the pumpkin grower.

Sorting and Classifying

If children have brought in pumpkins from home or have picked pumpkins on a field trip, use them for classifying and sorting activities. Ask children to write their names on their pumpkins with black markers. Have them sort the pumpkins by size, shape, with stem and with no stem, weight, color variations, and so on.

Class Visitor—Pumpkin Painters

Invite a parent or someone in the community who paints pumpkins to class. Check with a local garden or flower shop for help. Have them demonstrate their technique with paints and brushes. Then have pumpkins on hand for children to paint, too.

Fall Observations

Take the class on a neighborhood walk to look for signs of fall, such as changing leaves, birds flying south, a cool breeze. Invite children to record their observations by painting a fall mural.

Art Activities

Easel Paintings

If possible, bring in straw for children to use as paintbrushes. Bind the straw together, then let children create a fall scene with their fun new brushes. Display the paintings for all to enjoy.

Finger Paintings

Line a table with newspaper, art paper, and pots of orange paint. Invite children to finger paint their own jack-o'-lanterns. When dry, display the paintings to create a classroom pumpkin patch.

Scarecrow Creations

Divide the class into small groups. Have each group work cooperatively to create a paper scarecrow. Suggest that they first brainstorm a list of things they will need. Provide the groups with large sheets of oaktag or poster board, various pieces of construction paper, and fabric scraps. Have the groups decide which member will be responsible for which part of the scarecrow (shirt, pants, head, feet, and hands). Have students construct and glue their scarecrow pieces to the oaktag. Display the scarecrows with the finger-painted pumpkin patches.

Food Feasts Quilt

Students will learn to identify fruits and vegetables as they create this harvest quilt. Border squares reflect harvest colors, while the turkey hand-print patches gobble throughout. And fruit and vegetable patches add variety and detail. This pleasing class quilt is certain to be a visual feast for the eyes to savor.

Border Patch

Give each student a 9" x 9" (22.5 cm x 22.5 cm) purple construction-paper square, and sheets of red, orange, and yellow construction paper. Help children measure and cut out one 2 1/4" x 9" (approximately 5.5 cm x 22.5 cm) strip from each of the three colors. Ask children to glue the strips to the purple quilt patch. When placing the border patches on the quilt, alternate horizontal and vertical stripes.

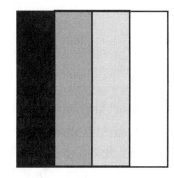

Fruits and Vegetables Patches

Invite children to create patches depicting fruits and vegetables. Give each child a white 9" x 9" (22.5 cm x 22.5 cm) square of construction paper. Have students paint or draw a favorite fruit or vegetable. For an artistic touch, invite children to cut out geometric shapes from scrap paper. Arrange the shapes to make fruits and vegetables and then glue to the patch.

Glyph Factor

Directions for making glyphs are found on page 6. Ask the children if they like eating turkey for Thanksgiving. Have the children record their answers on their Feast patches.

◆ If children like turkey, make a fruit patch.
◆ If children do not like turkey, make a vegetable patch.

Crow Patch

Have fun with this turkey hand-print patch. Invite each child to take turns painting the palm and thumb of one hand with brown paint. Continue by painting the fingers purple, red, yellow, and orange. Then help the child press his or her hand on a yellow 9" x 9" (22.5 cm x 22.5 cm) construction-paper patch. Once the patches have dried, invite each child to finish his or her turkey by drawing a beak, a wattle, and legs.

Literature Connections

Book Activity

Read the book *Growing Vegetable Soup,* by Lois Ehlert (Harcourt Brace, 1991). Point out the rhyming pattern of the text. Recite with the children their favorite pages. Ask them which vegetables they'd like to add to the soup. Would they like to make a fruit soup? Encourage children to substitute any vegetables or fruits not already mentioned in the story.

Pocket Chart

Sing this harvest food song, sung to the tune of "Frère Jacques." Write each line on sentence strips to place in your pocket chart, cutting apart the last word from the first two lines.

We eat corn,   *Always on Thanksgiving,*
We eat corn.   *Always on Thanksgiving.*
Oh so good!   *Yum, yum, yum.*
Oh so good!   *Yum, yum, yum.*

What else do children enjoy eating on Thanksgiving? Encourage them to substitute the word *corn* with other favorite foods. Write each food on a new sentence strip to replace the word *corn,* then sing the song again with the class. Other foods children might sing about include turkey, potatoes, stuffing, cranberries, salad, pumpkin pie, and so on.

Hanging Poem Chart

Share this poem about fruits and vegetables with the class.

Red, red apples,   *White white potatoes,*
Purple, purple plums,   *Green, green peas,*
Yellow, yellow bananas,   *Orange, orange carrots,*
Taste good when Thanksgiving comes!   *Fill my plate, if you please!*

Invite children to read the poem with you as you run your finger from left to right under each line. Ask children to point to the fruits and vegetables from the poem that appear on the class quilt. Assign a line to groups of children to perform as a choral reading.

Illustrated Student Book

Encourage children to create their own books about a feast. Provide children with several sheets of writing paper that include a blank space at the top or bottom. On each page, have children write the following sentence starter: "For a feast, you need _____ ." Encourage children to complete the sentences with the

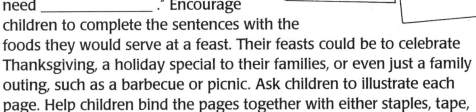

foods they would serve at a feast. Their feasts could be to celebrate Thanksgiving, a holiday special to their families, or even just a family outing, such as a barbecue or picnic. Ask children to illustrate each page. Help children bind the pages together with either staples, tape, or a three-hole punch and yarn. Invite children to share their books with their families.

Class Rolled Storybook

Read the book *The Hungry Thing,* by Jan Slepian and Ann Seidler (Scholastic, 1988). Discuss the silly things that happen in the story. Invite the class to retell the story by creating a rolled storybook. Using their own names, have children write a misunderstanding from the story. Encourage each student to turn his or her paper sideways. Invite them to illustrate their sentences. Tape the papers together, end to end, and roll up the entire length. Show the class how to unroll the pages to read the whole story.

Writing Journal

Which do children prefer—fruits or vegetables? Give children time to think about it, then encourage them to write their ideas in their journals. Invite the children to explain why they like fruits or vegetables. Have children give a brief description to support their preferences.

Writing Table

If you have fruit and vegetable ink stamps, display them on the writing table, along with small blank books. Instruct children to stamp fruits and vegetables on each page, then write simple sentences, such as "I see a carrot."

Math Activities

Graphing

Which fruits and vegetables are children's favorites? Create a bar graph to record the children's preferences. List each food in a column. Draw one fruit or vegetable next to the food for each vote. Ask the children which fruit is the most popular. Which vegetable? How can you tell? (The fruit and vegetable with the most pictures—usually the longest row—is the winner.)

Estimation

If you have fruit and vegetable math counters, place them in a jar and ask children to estimate the amount. Write students' guesses on the chalkboard. Invite children to help you count the fruits and vegetables in the jar to confirm the answer. Encourage children to estimate the number of grapes in a bunch, the number of strawberries or blueberries in a basket, or the number of raisins in a box. After you count the fruits, pass them out to children to eat. (As with any food activity, make sure no child has a food allergy.)

Survey

Divide the class into pairs. Invite children to survey their partners about their fruit and vegetable likes and dislikes. Assign a fruit or vegetable to each pair, have them write or draw it at the top of a sheet of paper. Show them how to make two columns—one headed "Yes," the other "No." With pencils in hand, have students mingle among their classmates, asking if they like the foods or not. Have them mark the answer by drawing a tally mark in the appropriate column. Invite children to count the marks to determine which foods classmates like and dislike. Share the results of the survey with the class.

"Concentration" Game

Using the "Concentration" game board (see instructions on page 6), create fruit and vegetable cards. Make sure you have ten pairs of matching foods. Review with children that they are to place the cards face down on the game board, then take turns flipping over two cards at a time. If the cards match, they remove the pair and continue. If not, it is the next player's turn. The game ends when all the cards have been removed. The player with the most pairs wins.

© Fearon Teacher Aids FE7947

"What's Missing?" Memory Game

Place an assortment of whole fruits and vegetables on a tray or plate. Invite the class to study the plate for about 30 seconds, then instruct children to close their eyes. Remove one or two foods and ask children to study the plate again. Challenge them to tell you which fruit or vegetable is missing. Continue until interest holds, making the game more challenging each time.

Measuring

Divide the class into small groups or pairs. Invite children to measure items using a cucumber. Lay the cucumber along desks, ledges, shelves, arms, and so on. Measure how many cucumbers it takes to cover the length of the different items. Have students write sentences to record their ideas, such as, "My leg measures 5 cucumbers. The dictionary measures 3 cucumbers."

Patterning

Invite children to cut up sponges in the shape of food items, such as round apples and oranges; triangular strawberries, carrots, and bunches of grapes; and oval lemons, watermelons, and cucumbers. Encourage children to dip the sponges into pans of paint and press them to paper to make patterns.

Science Activities

Sorting and Classifying

Place an assortment of fruits and vegetables—either real or plastic—into a bowl. Challenge children to sort them, for example, by color, size, fruit or vegetable, like it or dislike it, and so on.

Cooking

Make a fruit or vegetable salad in class. Combine small pieces of fruits or vegetables into a bowl, then spoon the mixture into paper cups. Pass out the cups and plastic spoons for children to sample.

Experiment

How do children think raisins might change when dropped into a glass of water? Invite children to find out. Give each student a raisin to hold and examine. What does the raisin feel like? What does it look like? Suggest that students draw the raisin in their science journals. Divide the class into small groups. Provide children with clear plastic cups of water. Have students drop their raisins into the water, then leave the cups overnight. The next morning, have groups observe their raisins, drawing what they see in their journals. Children should see that the water has made the raisins fluffy and larger, like grapes!

Tactile Table

Fill your tactile table with a variety of dried beans, peas, pasta, and corn. Encourage children to manipulate scoops, funnels, and other kitchen utensils to explore the dried foods.

Investigation

Locate a local farmer's market for children to visit. Encourage children to ask about the processes involved in planting, growing, harvesting, and preserving fruits and vegetables. Or, take a class field trip to a local grocery for a tour of the fruit-and-vegetable section. Many stores will let children taste more exotic fruits and vegetables. Back in class, invite children to draw pictures of themselves surrounded by the fruits and vegetables they investigated. Encourage the class to send a thank-you note to the proprietor of the store or market.

"Guess the Fruit" Game

How well do children think they know their fruits by smell? Invite children to play a game of "Guess the Fruit." Divide the class into small groups. Ask one student to close his or her eyes, while another group member holds a fruit up to his or her nose. Have a third child record the first child's answer. Have each group member identify a different fruit.

Observations

Give students several fruits and vegetables to observe. Encourage children to speculate what the insides of the different fruit or vegetable look like. Help them cut open the fruits and vegetables with plastic knives. Invite children to draw what they observe inside the fruit or vegetables in their science journals. Encourage them to pay attention to color, shape, and such details as seeds.

Art Activities

Easel Paintings

Arrange a bowl of fruit for students to paint. Then explain that still-life art is a popular form of painting. Set up easels, then invite the class to create their own still-life works of art. To display the artwork, create a bushel basket at the bottom of a bulletin board. Write the title "We're Learning in Bushels!" at the top of the board.

Clay Fruits and Vegetables

Provide students with modeling clay in different colors for children to mold fruits and vegetables. Place the clay figures in a cornucopia for a colorful harvest display.

Dramatic Play

Set up a "produce department" or "farmer's market" in an area of your class. Stock it with plastic fruits and vegetables. Use clean empty cans and cartons for frozen and preserved foods. Each food needs a price sticker. Encourage students to role-play being customers and merchants as they buy and sell fruits and vegetables.

The Pilgrims played an important role in American history. As students create Pilgrim patches and seaworthy *Mayflowers* they will discover this important era of America's past. The fancy turkey-feather border makes this a colorful quilt to treasure. This educational holiday project will stand as a symbol of class pride.

Border Patch

Provide several rolls of wrapping paper, or bring in wrapping paper you've used and saved. Encourage children to do the same. Invite students to draw and cut out colorful feathers from the wrapping paper to represent Thanksgiving turkeys. Have them glue the wrapping-paper feathers to a 9" x 9" (22.5 cm x 22.5 cm) light blue construction-paper square.

Pilgrim Patch

Share with children illustrations of Pilgrims from reference books and encyclopedias. Ask students what they think they would look like, dressed in Pilgrims' clothes? On a 9" x 9" (22.5 cm x 22.5 cm) white construction-paper patch, encourage students to draw self-portraits of themselves dressed as Pilgrims. Make sure children write their names on their patches. For younger children, provide a hat pattern for them to trace. For older students, suggest that they create their images with construction-paper scraps.

Glyph Factor

Directions for making glyphs are found on page 6. Ask the children if they would have liked to have been a Pilgrim. Have the children record their answers on their Pilgrim patches.

◆ If yes, create a black Pilgrim's hat.
◆ If no, create a dark blue Pilgrim's hat.
◆ If they're not sure, create a dark green Pilgrim's hat.

Mayflower Patch

Give each student a 9" x 9" (22.5 cm x 22.5 cm) light blue patch, pieces of green and blue tissue paper, and brown and white construction paper. Have children tear tissue paper into strips to create an ocean, gluing them to the bottom of the patch. Help children cut out boat shapes from brown paper and glue them to the ocean. Show them how to cut out square sails from white paper. Glue the sails above the ship and then draw the masts to connect them.

Literature Connections

Book Activity

Introduce the book *Thanksgiving Day,* by Gail Gibbons (Holiday House, 1983). Discuss with students the activities described in the book. Invite children to share what they do for Thanksgiving. Encourage children to freely express their Thanksgiving experiences.

Pocket Chart

Write the song below on oaktag sentence strips and place in the pocket chart. Teach children this song, sung to the tune "Row, Row, Row Your Boat."

Cook, cook, cook some turkey,
On Thanksgiving Day!
Think of all you're thankful for,
On this special day!

Encourage students to come up with other Thanksgiving-dinner activities to substitute for the words *cook* and *turkey* in the song. For example, mash some potatoes, pour some gravy, eat some stuffing, cut some pie, drink some milk, toss some salad, and so on.

Hanging Poem Chart

Write the following rhyme on the hanging chart.

I like food.
I like it a lot.
I like it cold.
I like it hot.
I like it chewy.
I like it crunchy.
I like it gooey.
Munchy! Munchy!

As students read the poem with you, be sure to track each line with a pointer or your finger. Then brainstorm other verses for the poem.

Class Holiday Food Book

Share the book *Feast for Ten,* by Cathryn Falwell (Houghton Mifflin, 1996). List the foods mentioned in the story. As a class, discuss the traditional foods served at their Thanksgiving dinners or other important holiday celebrations. Invite students to contribute to a holiday food book by drawing pictures of the foods they enjoy most at holiday time. Have children complete the sentence, "During the holidays, my family likes to eat _____ ." Ask the students to write their sentences in the holiday book. Assign volunteers to make a cover, then bind the pages together with staples or yarn. Encourage students to read the class book on their own.

Songs to Sing

Introduce Raffi's song "Apples and Bananas" (*One Light, One Sun,* MCA, 1996). This silly song is perfect for reviewing and practicing vowel sounds as children replace vowels in the words *apples* and *bananas.*

Writing Journal

Thanksgiving Day is a national holiday, when schools are closed and parents are home from work. Encourage children to write about Thanksgiving festivities in their journals. Prompt their writing with a sentence starter, such as, "On Thanksgiving, I will _____." When students return from the holiday, suggest that they write a sentence describing something special they did.

Writing Table

Share with children that long ago, people didn't write with pens or pencils, but instead with feathers dipped in ink! Present children with plastic feathers (check with a hobby or craft store). Show children how to dip the feathers in pots of paint, then challenge them to write their names or a message. As a class, discuss the experience.

Math Activities

Graphing

Ask students what are their favorite things about Thanksgiving. Is it the food? Or, visiting family and friends? Or, playing football? Or, perhaps even just a day off from school? What else do children do on this special day? Record children's answers on a bar graph. List the Thanksgiving activities on the graph, then draw a star or check mark for each child's vote. The row with the most marks is the most popular.

Estimation

Place a number of dried corn kernels in a jar. How many kernels do children think there are? Ask them to write their ideas on self-stick notes to display on the jar above the corn. Invite students to count the kernels to check their estimates. Whose estimate was closest?

Problem Solving

Ahead of time, create a turkey story board for children to manipulate. Draw a turkey on a sheet of oaktag, and cut out a dozen feathers. Ask students to solve turkey subtraction problems. For example, "This turkey has 10 feathers." (Have students count 10 feathers and place them on the turkey.) "Waddling through the forest, it bumped into a rock, and 3 feathers fell off." (Have students remove 3 feathers.) "How many feathers does the turkey have left?" Challenge students to write the equation, then count the feathers to determine the answer. (10 feathers − 3 feathers = 7 feathers)

"What's Missing?" Memory Game

Collect several Thanksgiving items and arrange them on a table. For example: a Pilgrim hat, a turkey picture, a football, a toy boat for the *Mayflower*, a pumpkin, a cornucopia (harvest horn), dried corn on the cob, or a piece of fruit. Discuss the items and their significance to the Thanksgiving holiday. Then have children close their eyes as you remove one or two items. Have children open their eyes and guess what is missing. Play additional rounds as interest holds.

Weighing

Have students weigh small items on a balance scale, such as paper clips, pencils, erasers, and a bookmark. Show the children how to place the items on one end of the scale and count out corn kernels onto the other end until the scale balances. Encourage children to record their answers by completing such sentences as, "One pencil weighs 7 corn kernels."

Patterning

Set up bowls of uncooked elbow and rigatoni macaroni in different colors. Invite the children to create patterned necklaces. Have them string the noodles on yarn, alternating the shapes and colors to form a pattern. Challenge classmates to recognize the patterns. Then suggest that the children give their noodle necklaces to a family member as a special holiday gift.

Science Activities

Experiment

Understanding how plants grow was very important to the Pilgrims because they had to grow their own food. Try this experiment to show children how plants "carry" water and nutrients through their stems to the leaves.

Divide the class into small groups. Give each group a celery stalk, slit in half at the bottom. Help groups place one side of the celery in a cup of water mixed with blue food coloring, and the other end in a cup of water mixed with red food coloring. What do students predict will happen? Over a 24-hour period, they should notice that the colored water travels up the celery stalk to the leaves. Encourage them to conclude that the stem of a plant transports water to its leaves.

Snack Comparisons

Have a variety of different cranberry foods available for children to sample, such as cranberry sauce, cranberry juice, and cranberry bread. Invite students to taste and compare the foods, perhaps taking a class vote on which form they enjoy most.

Investigation

Three hundred years ago, the Pilgrims sailed from England to the shores of the new world. Ask students if they have ever wondered how such large and heavy boats were able to float across the Atlantic Ocean. Help them with this experiment to find out. Show students two equal slabs of clay. As the children watch, shape one into a compact ball and the other into a boat. Fill a plastic tub with water, and ask students to predict which will float and which will sink. Children should observe that the ball sinks, but the boat floats. Ask students how this is possible, when they are both made of the same amount of clay. Explain that it has to do with how much water the object pushes aside, or displaces. The ball doesn't push aside much water. It weighs more than the water it pushes aside, so the ball sinks. But the boat takes up more space, so it pushes aside more water. The water it pushes aside weighs more than the boat, so the boat floats.

Tactile Table

Cover a table with newspaper, and fill several plastic tubs of water for students to experiment with. Provide materials for making other boats, such as foil, sponges, cork, cups, plastic butter containers, and bars of soap.

Science Journal

Place a cob of dried corn or Indian corn in your Feely Box. (see instructions on page 7.) Invite students to explore the Feely Box and to think about the object inside. Encourage them to describe the object in their science or writing journals. Invite the students to guess what's in the box. Then reveal the corn cob to the class.

Art Activities

Easel Paintings

Provide children with paint and art paper. Invite them to paint the *Mayflower* sailing the high seas. You might have illustrations of the *Mayflower* on hand for children to use as examples. Display the paintings around the room.

"Fruit O" Turkeys

Pass out drawing paper. Ask students to draw a turkey's body. Then set out bowls of "Fruit O" cereal. Invite students to glue cereal around the body to create colorful turkey feathers.

Computer Art

If a computer is available to your class, invite students to create a menu for a Thanksgiving dinner. Help them type dinner items, then use clip art and borders to decorate the menus. Encourage students to print out their menus to compare with those of their classmates.

December Eve Quilt

Santa Claus and his eight flying reindeer are a holiday tradition that appeals to most children, no matter their heritage. This holiday quilt features Santa and his deer, along with other ways to celebrate the winter holidays. To truly get students into the holiday spirit, play some fun holiday music as children create their quilt patches.

Border Patch

Give each student a 9" x 9" (22.5 cm x 22.5 cm) black construction-paper square. Tell them to randomly drizzle the patch with glue, then to dip the patch into gold glitter. Students will have created a beautiful nighttime backdrop for the winter trees. Cut two 7" (17.5 cm) green triangles and one 2" (5 cm) brown square from construction paper for the trees. Glue the trees on top of the glitter background.

Encourage those children who do not celebrate Christmas to make patches showing other symbols of holiday celebrations, such as a menorah for Hanukkah or a kinara for Kwanza, and so on.

Glyph Factor

Directions for making glyphs are found on page 6. The glyph factor for this activity has already been determined by the special holiday item each child created on the border patch.

Santa Patch

Invite children to create three-dimensional Santa patches. Provide each student with red, white, and pink construction paper, cotton balls, and a 9" x 9" (22.5 cm x 22.5 cm) green quilt patch. Encourage children to make Santa heads from the materials and use cotton balls for the white trim of his hat. Invite children to glue the pieces to the green square. Have them complete the patch by curling 4-inch (10 cm) strips of white paper into a fluffy beard and glue to Santa's chin.

Reindeer Patch

To make the reindeer patch, have children dip a hand into brown paint, then press it to a 9" x 9" (22.5 cm x 22.5 cm) white quilt patch. After they clean their hands and the painted reindeer have dried, ask each child to glue on chenille-stem antlers, a pom-pom nose, a cottonball tail, and a red ribbon around the reindeer's neck. Make sure children write their names on their patches, too.

Literature Connections

Book Activity

Share the book *The Shoemaker and the Elves,* by Paul Galdone (Clarion Books, 1984). Discuss how the shoemaker's elves might remind the children of Santa's helpers. Encourage children to imagine that they are elves. Who would they like to help? If they could help Santa, which tasks would they do? Invite children to write and illustrate sentences expressing their ideas. For example, "If Ramon were an elf, he would help his grandmother with her yard work." "If Katera were an elf, she would help feed Santa's reindeer."

Pocket Chart

How would students describe Santa Claus? Create a pocket chart to help them sing about Santa's distinguishing attributes. Copy this song onto oaktag sentence strips, then teach it to the class. It is sung to the tune of "London Bridge Is Falling Down."

Santa has a big, red hat,
big, red hat,
big, red hat!
Santa has a big, red hat,
Doesn't he look great?

Encourage children to substitute the words *big, red hat* for *cherry nose, two shiny boots, big round belly*, or *snowy beard*.

Hanging Song Chart

Invite children to share holiday songs, including those special to their families. Write the words of a holiday song on a hanging chart, such as "Jingle Bells." Sing this song several times, adding a horse each time. Encourage children to sing faster, for a "three-horse" open sleigh moves faster than a "one-horse" open sleigh. Supply bells for students to add sound effects.

"A Season of Lights" Class Book

Point out to children that many winter celebrations include lights. For example, Christmas trees are adorned with lights. Seven candles are lit during Kwanza. Hanukkah is celebrated by lighting nine candles over eight days. In Germany, an Advent wreath bears four red candles. And during the nine evenings of Mexican Las Posadas, families carry candles as they walk from home to home and sing. Find books about these traditions to read with the class. Encourage students to share their own family experiences. Ask them to draw and illustrate the special ways they celebrate the winter holidays. Encourage children to draw the lights their families use to celebrate, including decorations and candles. Combine the pages for a class book titled "A Season of Lights."

"Rudolph" Mini-Theater

Invite children to act out the song "Rudolph, the Red-Nosed Reindeer." Gather two red Santa's hats, several green elf hats, red dot stickers, and black dot stickers. Make antlers out of brown oaktag taped to a plastic headband. Assign roles to the children. Have the children playing Santa and his wife wear red hats, the elves wear green hats, the reindeer wear black dot stickers on their noses, and Rudolph wear a red dot sticker on his or her nose. (As with all roles, do not limit the parts by gender.) Invite the class to sing the song "Rudolph the Red-Nosed Reindeer" and act it out. Encourage children to switch roles if they wish.

Writing Journal

The holidays are an exciting time, full of many things to do. Gifts need to be bought, cookies baked, presents wrapped, and decorations hung. Ask students what other things they need to do. Encourage them to write "to-do" lists in their writing journals. When children return to school after the winter break, ask them to review their lists to see if they successfully completed their tasks.

Writing Table

Collect a variety of gift tags to place on your writing table. Show children how to fill them out by writing their names after the word "From" and the person's name to whom they wish to give a gift after the word "To." Or, provide drawing paper for children to create their own tag designs.

© Fearon Teacher Aids FE7947

Math Activities

Graphing

Ask students which winter holiday activities are their favorites—exchanging gifts, making decorations, singing holiday songs, visiting with relatives and friends, making presents, or baking cookies. Make a chart with columns for each holiday activity. Label the columns with the holiday activities. Then ask children to write their names under the things they like to do most. Have children choose two favorite activities. Then ask them to look at the chart and identify which holiday activity is the most popular.

Counting

Create a holiday bell to help children count down the days remaining until winter vacation. Cut a bell from oaktag and cover it with gift wrap. Loop construction-paper strips in holiday colors to form a chain. Glue the chain to the bottom of the bell. At the end of each day, have a child ring a real bell, then ask another child to cut off one loop from the chain. Ask a third child to count the remaining loops and announce how many days are left until winter vacation. Record the number on the chalkboard.

Estimation

Read the book *The Shoemaker and the Elves,* by Paul Galdone (Clarion, 1984), and place a number of toy shoes in a jar. Ask children how many shoes the elves have made. Write their estimates on the chalkboard. Invite several children to help count the shoes, and circle the number on the chalkboard that comes closest.

Problem Solving

Suggest to children that they are Santa's record keepers, then pose problems for them to solve. For example, "The children in the Smith family have asked for 2 dolls, 4 trains, and 6 books. How many presents must Santa deliver?" Or, "The elves have 12 orders for in-line skates. They've made 7. How many more skates do they still need to make?" Write word problems on index cards, and place them in a holiday basket to keep in the math center. Ask children to write down the math equations, drawing pictures of the items to aid in problem solving.

"What's Missing?" Memory Game

Display six to eight holiday items—for example, a wreath, wrapping paper, bows, gift tags, ornaments, holiday miniatures, a menorah, and so on. Discuss the various objects. Ask students to close their eyes as you remove one or two items. When children open their eyes, challenge them to figure out what item is missing. Continue the game, each time making it more challenging.

Measuring

Bring in evergreen boughs for children to use as measuring tools. Give the boughs to groups or partners, then ask them to find objects that are similar in length. Encourage children to write sentences to describe their findings. For example, "This toy truck is as long as this bough." "The bough is 12 inches (30 cm) long."

Patterning

Cut 1-inch (2.5 cm) squares from three different holiday wrapping papers. Have children arrange the squares to create patterns. Glue the squares to sentence strips, then write out the pattern sequence for others to recognize.

Science Activities

Observation

Most trees lose their leaves during winter. But not evergreens, or coniferous trees. If conifers are available in your area, invite children to observe them. How are their leaves different from deciduous trees? How does this help them? (The leaves are tougher and they can still make food. The waxy texture prevents the leaves from drying out.) Have children draw pictures of the different leaves in their science journals.

Encourage children to notice any animals they observe in the evergreen tree, such as birds, insects, and small mammals. Read the book *A Cobweb Christmas,* by Shirley Climo (HarperCollins, 1982), and discuss other animals that make their homes in evergreens.

Weighing

Show students how to weigh small classroom items on a balance scale using pine cones for weight. Place the object on one end, then ask students to count out the number of pine cones necessary to balance the scale. Have students record their findings in their science journals. For example, "One small book weighs as much as 10 pine cones."

Experiment

If possible, bring pine boughs to class and set them in jars of water to keep fresh. Remind children to replace the water every few days. Suggest that children record the amount of water the boughs "drink." (You might also bring in baby evergreens for children to water, too. Check with a local nursery or flower shop.)

Discuss which type of water might be best for your boughs or trees. Have students give the plants different water, for example, salt water, sugar water, water mixed with aspirin, and ordinary water. Suggest that children draw each tree to notice any differences.

Investigation

If possible, set up a field trip to a park with evergreens. Check with your local park service or the National Audubon Society for programs in your area. Many parks offer tours for children. Encourage children to note various sizes, numbers, and formations of branches, tree sap, and tree rings. After returning to class, discuss the things the children enjoyed most, then invite them to express their thoughts in thank-you letters to the park.

Classification

Provide students with nature magazines. Have them cut out pictures of different kinds of trees. Help children classify the trees—deciduous or coniferous. Start a two-column chart, asking students to glue the tree pictures in the appropriate columns.

Art Activities

Easel Paintings

Set up easels for children to paint festive holiday scenes. Suggest that they paint Santa and his reindeer, a festival of lights, or something special to them about the holidays. To make their artwork really "shine," encourage them to sprinkle the paintings with glitter while the paint is still a bit damp. The sparkles will stick, adding an extra holiday sparkle.

Wonderful Wreaths

Help children draw a medium-sized circle on a sheet of art paper. Then show them how to dip a sponge glass washer into green paint, then press it lightly along the circle. The sponge glass washer will make a lovely evergreen, boughlike print. Encourage students to cut a bow from wrapping paper to complete their wreaths.

Gingerbread Treat Quilt

Sweeten up your December studies with this tasty gingerbread quilt. Wrapped-candy borders accent gingerbread children. Building gingerbread houses makes the treat complete. Sugar and spice and gingerbread nice—that's what this cooperative quilt is made of!

Border Patch

Create paper candies for a fun-looking border. Provide each student with a 9" x 9" (22.5 cm x 22.5 cm) white construction-paper patch, a red circle to fit in the center, and two small triangles. Show children how to arrange the pieces to resemble wrapped candies, then glue them in place.

Glyph Factor

Directions for making glyphs are found on page 6. Ask the children how their families are going to spend the winter holidays. Some families might take vacations, others might visit relatives, and still others might just stay home. What are your students doing? Encourage children to share their plans by painting dots on their candies.

- ◆ If children are staying home, paint five dots.
- ◆ If children are visiting relatives, paint ten dots.
- ◆ If children are going on vacation, paint twenty dots.

Gingerbread Child Patch

Create gingerbread-child patterns large enough to fill a 9"x 9" (22.5 cm x 22.5 cm) white square. Have children trace the pattern onto tan or brown construction paper and cut it out. Provide plastic glitter snowflakes for students to glue on to represent frosting. Ask them to draw in facial features, then suggest that they cut out and glue on bows and ties from fabric scraps.

Gingerbread House Patch

Pass out a 9" x 9" (22.5 cm x 22.5 cm) pink construction-paper patch to each student. Have them cut house shapes from tan or brown construction paper to glue to the patch. Supply them with cotton balls, small round candies, and plastic snow to decorate their houses.

Literature Connections

Book Activity

The story of "The Gingerbread Boy" is a traditional holiday treat. Locate several different versions in children's anthologies to share with the class. Challenge students to compare and contrast the various retellings, discussing characters, setting, dialogue, and plot twists. Set up a flannelboard for children to tell their own versions of "The Gingerbread Boy."

Pocket Chart

Write these rhyming lines on sentence strips to place in your pocket chart.

Run, run, as fast as you can.
You can't catch me.
I'm the gingerbread man!

Brainstorm with children other verbs to substitute for the word *run*, such as *skip, hop, crawl, fly, jump, leap, dance, gallop,* and so on. Replace the word *run* with a new word strip, then recite the new rhyme with the class.

Hanging Poem Chart

Invite the class to be part of this gingerbread counting rhyme. Write the rhyme on the hanging chart, leaving blank spaces for children's names. Ask students to read the rhyme along with you. Have children raise their hands if they would like to "bake another one," then choose a child to write his or her name within the line. Pause before the end of each verse for children to supply the new number of cookies.

One yummy gingerbread boy,
With a tie of blue.
Billy bakes another one.
Now there are two.

Two yummy gingerbread boys,
By the winter tree.
Addie bakes another one.
Now there are three.

Three yummy gingerbread boys,
With sprinkles galore.
Taylor bakes another one.
Now there are four.

Four yummy gingerbread boys,
They almost look alive!
Lisa bakes another one.
Now there are five.

For other verses, use the following words:
Five/Which one should I pick? Six/They taste like heaven; Seven/Their frosting looks great; Eight/Which one is mine? Nine/They look like little men.

"The Gingerbread Boy" Class Book

Speculate with children holiday objects the gingerbread boy might run away from—for example, reindeer, a snowflake, a wreath. Have children write a sentence and illustrate it. For example, "Hannah's gingerbread boy ran away from Rudolph." Assign a group to make a cover with the title "The Gingerbread Boy Story." Bind the pages together and invite the class to read their new tale along with you.

"Sing and Move" Chant

Clear a space in the classroom for children to move around. Then teach them this chant, encouraging them to act out the motions. Brainstorm other verses to continue your "Cookie Boy and Girl" chants.

Cookie boy, cookie boy,
Turn around, round, round.
Cookie girl, cookie girl,
Touch the ground, ground, ground.
Cookie boy, cookie boy,
Reach up high, high, high.
Cookie girl, cookie girl,
Blink your eye, eye, eye.

Writing Journal

The smell of gingerbread is almost magical, conjuring up warm, cozy images. Ask children if they have ever smelled gingerbread before. Encourage children who have smelled it to describe the scent. Place some gingerbread in cups to pass around for children to sniff. Have children write about what the smell of gingerbread reminds them of. Then eat the gingerbread! Yum!

Writing Table

If you have rubber stamps or cookie cutters in the shapes of gingerbread cookies or houses, place them on your writing table. Encourage students to use the stamps or to trace the cookie cutters onto sheets of paper, then to write their own cookie stories.

Math Activities

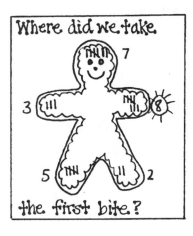

Graphing

Draw a large gingerbread boy or girl on a sheet of chart paper. Pass out gingerbread cookies, and invite each child to take one bite. Where did children take their first bites? Did they bite off the right arm? A left leg? The head? Place tally marks on the appropriate body part on your chart. Which part of the cookie did students eat first?

Estimation

Ask children how many bites students estimate it will take to finish one gingerbread cookie. Have them write down their guesses, then pass out a cookie for each child to eat. Stress that they shouldn't "force" their estimates by taking bigger or smaller bites than normal. Have children draw a tally mark for each bite, then count the marks to check their estimates.

Problem Solving

Encourage children to imagine they are master bakers, baking gingerbread cookies. Suggest such problems as, "Mrs. Jones ordered 4 gingerbread cookies. Mr. White ordered 7 cookies. How many cookies do you need to bake?" Write the word problems on index cards to store on cookie sheets. Encourage children to use clay to mold the number of cookies in each problem to help solve it.

"Guess My Category" Game

Gather the ingredients needed to make gingerbread, such as a bag of flour, a carton of eggs, sprinkles, frosting, sugar, and a carton of milk. Place the items in a bag, along with other ingredients or objects not pertaining to baking gingerbread. Create two circles labeled "Yes" and "No." Take out the flour and place it in the "Yes" circle. Can children guess the category? Continue pulling items from the bag, asking students in which circle they belong. When all the items have been sorted, challenge students to conclude that all the items in the "Yes" circle are ingredients for gingerbread.

Measuring Volume

Fill three plastic peanut-butter jars with different amounts of flour. Can students tell which jar has more? Have children use the same-sized scoops to spoon out flour, counting each scoop. Have children write less-than (<) and more-than (>) equations. For example: Jar 1= 5 scoops. Jar 2 = 8 scoops. Then 5 scoops < 8 scoops.

Patterning

Create reproducibles of gingerbread boys and gingerbread girls. Then challenge children to create an AABB pattern alternating the boy-girl patterns. Encourage children to create their own pattern sequences, too.

Science Activities

Observation/Cooking

Select a gingerbread recipe to prepare in class. Invite children to help whenever possible. Encourage them to notice how ingredients change. For example, flour doesn't change much if mixed with sugar, but it becomes doughy when mixed with water or milk. After baking, slice the gingerbread and pass it out for children to try. Encourage children to frost and decorate the gingerbread, too.

Taste Comparisons

Many of the ingredients for making gingerbread are white. Fill cups with sugar, salt, baking soda, flour, and powdered sugar, and invite children to taste each ingredient. Have them come up with adjectives to describe the differences, such as sweet or salty; coarse or fine; good tasting or bad tasting.

Experiment

Different foods mix differently with water. These are basic chemical reactions. Invite children to mix water with salt and water with sugar to see what happens. Add food coloring to differentiate the two cups—stir in blue food coloring to the sugar solution and red food coloring to the salt solution. For best results use one cup (240 ml) of water for one teaspoon (5 ml) of sugar or salt. Invite children to draw what happens in their science journals.

Investigation

Plan a field trip to a local bakery. Discuss with the children the things they expect to see at the bakery. During the trip, have children ask the baker questions. Back in class, review the children's expectations for the trip and discuss any surprising things they learned. Make sure to send a thank-you note to the baker, perhaps including children's illustrations of things they enjoyed most.

Classification

Which foods do children think are sweet? Which are sour? Start a two-column chart for children to record their ideas. Have children draw pictures of different foods and place them in the appropriate columns. Or, suggest that they flip through magazines to find pictures of foods. Continue the chart by adding salty and spicy foods, too.

Class Visitor—Baker

If a field trip to a local bakery isn't possible, invite a baker to visit. Besides pastry bakers, you might try a pizzeria, too. Invite the pizza maker to show children how dough is molded and twirled to make pie shapes, then cooked with favorite toppings.

Art Activities

Stuffed Gingerbread Figures

Create a large gingerbread-child pattern. Pass out brown paper for children to fold in half. Have students trace the pattern and cut out both gingerbread figures. On one cutout, ask children to paint facial features and frosting details. Then staple both cutouts together, leaving an opening at the bottom. Show children how to stuff the figures with tissue or newspaper, then staple the bottoms closed.

Cinnamon-Applesauce Clay Figures

For each student, mix 1 cup (240 ml) of ground cinnamon, 3/4 cup (180 ml) of unsweetened applesauce, and 2 tablespoons (30 ml) of white glue. Show children how to knead the mixture for about two to three minutes until smooth. Help children roll the dough into a 1/4-inch thickness (about half a centimeter). Then pass out cookie cutters for children to create "gingerbread" figures. Place the cutouts on a cookie sheet, and let air dry for two to three days.

Dramatic Play

Invite the class to act out their own theatrical production of "The Gingerbread Boy." Assign roles and tasks to the children. Besides acting out story characters, they can create murals for scenery, sound effects, costumes, and props. Once children feel confident with their production, invite them to share their performance with another class or with their families.

Winter Snow Quilt

No matter the weather in your part of the country, you can turn your classroom into a winter wonderland with this cooperative quilt. Children will not only create torn-paper snowmen, but their very own snowflakes. And the geometric snowflake border complements the winter motif. If the legendary Frosty could visit your quilt, he'd plan to stay year 'round!

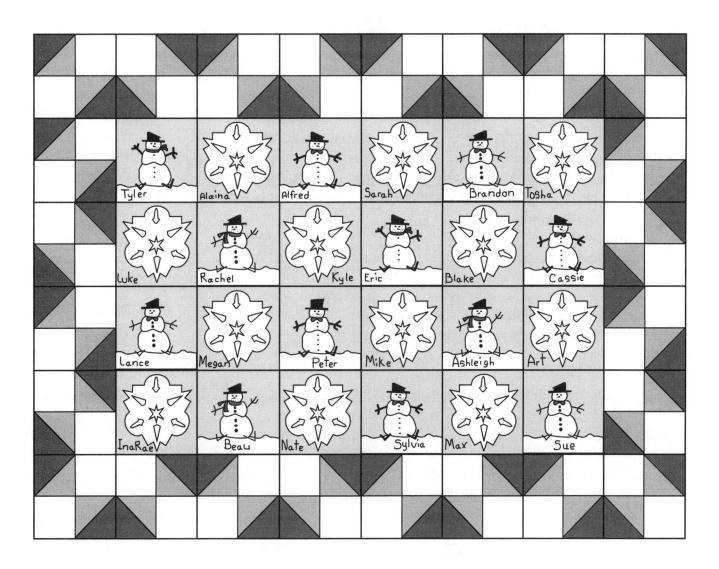

Border Patch

Give each student a 9" x 9" (22.5 cm x 22.5 cm) white patch of construction paper. Show them how to divide the square into four equal sections. Help children divide the top left square and the bottom right square in half by drawing diagonal lines, from the bottom left corner to the top right. Then have students color the outer triangles dark blue and the inner triangles light blue.

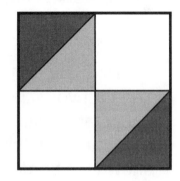

Snowman Patch

Encourage children to make torn-paper snowmen on a 9" x 9" (22.5 cm x 22.5 cm) light blue patch. Invite students to tear strips of white paper and glue them to the bottom of the patch to form the landscape. Then tear three circles from white paper and arrange them into a snowman. Glue the circles in place. Create a hat, arms, and facial features from dark-colored torn paper. Suggest that students use white crayons to add snowflakes.

Glyph Factor

Directions for making glyphs are found on page 6. Ask the children which snow activities they have experienced. If snow is not common in your area, have students choose one or all three of the activities they would like to try.

- ◆ If students would like to try sledding, draw a red scarf on their snowmen.
- ◆ If students would like to try building a snowman, draw a yellow scarf on their snowmen.
- ◆ If students would like to try skiing, draw a green scarf on their snowmen.
- ◆ If students would like to try all three, draw a pink scarf on their snowmen.

Snowflake Patch

Provide each student with circles measuring slightly under 9 inches (22.5 cm) in diameter. Show them how to fold the circles in half, then into thirds. This will make a six-sided design. Encourage students to snip small shapes from each folded area. Have students unfold their snowflakes to reveal their unique snowflake designs. Provide 9" x 9" (22.5 cm x 22.5 cm) red quilt patches for students to glue their snowflakes on.

Literature Connections

Book Activity

Read the book *Snowballs* by Lois Ehlert (Harcourt Brace, 1996). Discuss the interesting things the children see in the book. Encourage students to create their own snowmen. Provide a variety of materials for them to try, such as white pillowcases, fabric scraps, cotton balls, plastic-foam balls, clay, pint-size milk cartons, and cotton swabs. Challenge children to be as creative as possible, then display their snowmen as you read the book again.

Pocket Chart

Write the following rhyme on sentence strips.

5 little snowmen made of snow.
One had a hat and a big blue bow.
Out came the sun and shone all day.
Till one little snowmen melted away.

Suggest that students substitute other numbers and colors to change the rhyme. For example, 4 and yellow; 3 and red; 2 and orange; 1 and green, each time subtracting one snowman from the original five.

Hanging Poem Chart

Write the following rhyme on a hanging chart.

A silly little snowman had a carrot nose.
Along came a rabbit, and what do you suppose?
That hungry little rabbit, looking for some lunch
Ate that little snowman's nose-Nibble, Nibble, Crunch!

Brainstorm with students other animals that might visit the snowman and the foods they might eat. Rewrite the poem on your hanging chart to reflect children's ideas. For example: apple and horse; pickle and child; monkey and banana; or cookie and bird.

"Find the Snowballs" Class Book.

Distribute magazines for children to cut up. Have them cut out an object in which they'd like to hide a snowball. Ask children to glue the picture to a book page and then glue a cotton ball either under, above, beside, or "inside" (on top of the magazine picture). Encourage each child to write a sentence about the snowball. For example, "Rosa hid her snowball under the wagon." To complete each page, ask children to draw themselves in the scene. Encourage volunteers to create a cover with the leading sentence "See if you can find where we've hidden the snowballs." Share the class book with others.

Writing Journal

Place a wool mitten, scarf, or hat in your Feely Box. (see instructions on page 7). Invite children to describe the item in their journals. Ask them if they can tell which article of clothing it is. Have children draw pictures of themselves wearing the winter item. Invite each child to write a sentence about why this piece of clothing is helpful in the snow or cold weather.

Writing Table

Set up a table with black construction paper, snowflake stickers, rubber stamps, white paint, and white crayons. Have children create several snowflake designs on the paper. Encourage each child to write a sentence in white crayon about his or her snowy picture.

Math Activities

Graphing

Invite children to record snowfalls around the country on a bar graph. Over several weeks, check for headlines about wintry weather in your area and across the United States. Write the inches or centimeters on the vertical axis of the graph, with the names of cities along the horizontal axis. Then draw in the number of inches or centimeters of snow the area received. Ask children to study the chart to determine which place had the most snow.

Estimation

Fill your estimation jar with white cotton balls. Ask students to guess how many cotton balls they see. Record the children's estimates on self-stick notes and place on the jar. Ask a pair of students to count the cotton balls and to announce which classmate's estimate was the closest.

Real-World Math-Calendar Days

Show children different months of a calendar, and ask what they all have in common. Confirm that each day has a number. Invite the class to create its own calendar for the winter month you are currently in. Draw a large grid on poster board, with five rows of seven days each. Make sure you write the days, Sunday through Saturday, across the top of the calendar. Then ask children to fill in the numbers, or dates, for each day. Refer to a current calendar to make sure the dates fall on the correct days of the week. Help the children read the calendar by asking what today's date is. Then ask the children what the date is two days from now. Next week? Glue the class calendar to the bottom of a larger sheet of dark paper, and encourage children to create a wintry scene at the top with torn-paper and white crayons.

"Guess My Category" Game

Gather together the things needed to build a snowman, such as a scarf, small branches for arms, a hat, perhaps gloves, a carrot nose, and button eyes. Also include items that would never be used for a snowman. Place everything in a paper grocery bag. Create two circles on the floor or table with yarn or chalk, and label one circle "Yes" and the other "No." Pull out a snowman object from the bag and place it in the "Yes" circle. Take out other items, each time asking the students' advice on which circle to place the item in. Challenge children to guess what all the "yes" items have in common. When all the items have been sorted, confirm that the category is, indeed, items for building a snowman.

Measuring

Scarves make wonderful measuring tools. Working in groups, have children use scarves to measure long classroom items, such as a chalkboard ledge, a bulletin board, a book shelf (both height and length), the teacher's desk, the doorway, a closet, even the length and width of the classroom. Help the children lay the scarves end to end, and write the measurements. For example, "The length of the classroom equals 8 1/2 scarves."

Patterning

Provide students with white construction-paper mitten shapes. Invite students to draw patterned designs with markers and crayons. Divide the class into small groups. Encourage each group to come up with simple pattern sequences using the finished mittens. Challenge the other groups to identify the patterns.

Science Activities

Experiment

What happens when snow melts? Ask the children if they think the water from the melted snow takes up as much space as the snow. Encourage children to experiment to find out. Fill a clear plastic cup with water. Fill a second cup up to the same level as the first cup with crushed ice cubes or snow from outdoors. Draw a mark on the cup to show the level of the snow. As the ice or snow melts, have children notice the water level. Usually the water level of the melted ice or snow will be lower than the water in the other cup. Explain that although the snow or ice might have taken up as much space as the water, it was actually made from less water, so the water level from the melted snow was lower.

Food Fun

Invite children to make a healthy, snowman-shaped snack. Pass out a paper plate with two bread slices to each child. Tell them to shape the bread into the snowman's body. Then set up cups of other foods for children to use as the snowmen's features, such as raisins, nuts, banana slices, chocolate chips, strawberries, and grapes. Have children show their edible snowmen to classmates, then eat!

Experiment

Ask the children if they know what an ocean current is. Explain that ocean currents have to do with hot and cold water. Usually as cold water sinks, warmer water is pushed upward. Encourage children to experiment with colored ice cubes to see this phenomenon firsthand. Fill an ice-cube tray with water, and mix in some red or blue food coloring. Fill a clear tub or aquarium with hot water. Drop in the colored ice cubes. Encourage children to observe and then draw the swirling colors as the ice cubes melt. Point out that the colder water sinks, then rises as it warms up.

As a variation, freeze water mixed with many different color combinations of food coloring. As the colored ice cubes melt in the warm water, students will see an amazing variety of different swirling colors.

Investigation/Graphing

Invite children to investigate temperatures around the country. Write the temperature degrees on the vertical axis and place names of cities on the horizontal axis. Then help children look in newspapers to locate the temperatures for cities around the country. Have children plot the temperatures on a bar graph, then interpret the information to learn where the weather is the warmest and the coldest.

Classification

Provide an assortment of mittens and gloves for students to sort or classify. For example, they could classify them by color, size, patterns, and gloves or mittens.

Class Visitor—Meteorologist

Your students might not understand why it snows, but a meteorologist certainly does! Contact a local television or radio station to inquire if their weather person or meteorologist would be interested in visiting your class. Have him or her explain how snow and other types of weather are formed. Invite students to prepare a list of questions. Encourage your visitor to display maps and other fun tools of weather reporting. As a class, write a thank-you letter to send to your weather expert.

Art Activities

Cooperative Snowmen

Divide the class into cooperative groups of four to five students each. Invite them to work together to create a large snowman. Have children assign tasks, deciding which group member will be responsible for each part. For example, one student could make the head, another the body, another the arms, another the hat or scarf. Supply each group with a length of butcher paper to draw their snowman. Make sure students write their names near the body parts they created. Display the snowmen on a bulletin board to create an entire family of snow people.

Snowman Prints

Show students how to finger paint a white snowman on a cookie sheet. Cover the snowman painting with dark paper and press gently. Then carefully remove the paper. A snowman print should appear. Encourage children to try it themselves. Allow the prints to dry, then display them around the room.

Model Snowmen

Provide children with modeling clay. Encourage them to mold snowmen figures. Suggest that they use toothpicks for arms and construction paper for hats. Invite children to take their snowmen home to share with their families.

Video

To complete the exploration of snowy weather, invite children to watch the video *The Snowman,* by Raymond Briggs (PBS Productions). Discuss the film with the children. Did they enjoy it? What were their favorite parts? How might they continue the story? Encourage children to draw pictures and write sentences showing something they might do with a snowman friend.

Whatever the Weather Quilt

Expose children to the wonders of weather with this cooperative quilt. The stunning border in colors of gray, black, and blue will draw viewers into your weather world, where they will be delighted by patches that depict sunshine, snow, fog, wind, clouds, frost, and rain. This cooperative quilt forecasts pleasant viewing days ahead!

Border Patch

Give each student a gray 9" x 9" (22.5 cm x 22.5 cm) patch, along with four 3" x 3" (7.5 cm x 7.5 cm) blue squares and three 3" x 3" (7.5 cm x 7.5 cm) black squares. (To practice math skills, have the children measure and cut out the squares themselves.) Invite children to cut two black squares in half diagonally, creating triangles. Help children arrange the squares and triangles on the gray patch, following the border-patch illustration.

Sunshine Patch

Pass out light blue 9" x 9" (22.5 cm x 22.5 cm) quilt patches. Ask students to draw a small circle in the center of the patch to represent the sun. Have children dip their fingers into yellow or orange paint and press them around the sun to create sun rays. Their fingers should point outward, toward the edge of the patch.

Glyph Factor

Directions for making glyphs are found on page 6. Ask the children if they have ever seen a rainbow. Have the children record their answers on their sun patches.

- ◆ If students have seen a rainbow, paint the sun rays yellow.
- ◆ If students have not seen a rainbow, paint the sun rays orange.

Wind Patch

Sprinkle gray enamel paint into a pan of water. Then ask students to slide 9" x 9" (22.5 cm x 22.5 cm) gray quilt patches on top of the water to capture a windy pattern. Encourage students to make kites from construction paper to glue to their wind patches.

Precipitation Patches

The precipitation patches will vary. Have children work in groups to create the different patches. Start by giving the groups 9" x 9" (22.5 cm x 22.5 cm) gray construction-paper squares. Ask them to complete the following directions on page 83 to illustrate fog, rain, frost, snow, and cloud patches.

Fog Patch

Invite students to draw a winter hillside scene, complete with barren trees with dark-colored markers or crayons. Invite children to measure and cut out a 9" x 9" (22.5 cm x 22.5 cm) square of white tissue paper, then glue edges to the patch. This will create a foggy effect.

Rain Patch

Help students fill an eye dropper with watered down blue paint. Drip several drops across the top of the gray patch. Have students stand their patches upright to let the drops drizzle down the paper, resembling raindrops on a windowpane. Allow the patch to dry before handling.

Frost Patch

Invite students to draw a winter scene pressing firmly with crayons on their gray patches. Mix a water-and-Epsom-salt solution for students to paint over their pictures. Set the patches aside to dry. When dry, the Epsom-salt solution will look like winter frost.

Snow Patch

Give each student two to three white circles measuring about 3 inches (7.5 cm) in diameter. Have students fold the circles in half, then in thirds. Encourage them to cut out small shapes around the edges of the circles. Ask them to unfold the circles to reveal the beautiful snowflakes. Encourage children to glue their one-of-a kind snowflakes to their gray quilt patches.

Cloud Patch

Show children how to fold their gray quilt patches in half, and drop two teaspoons (10 ml) of white paint into the middle. Demonstrate how to fold the patch and rub the paper. Invite them to open the patch to see the cloud formations they have made.

Literature Connections

Book Activity

Read the book *Cloudy With a Chance of Meatballs,* by Judi Barrett (Simon & Schuster, 1982). Discuss the funny things the weather brings in the story. Encourage children to write a silly class weather book, illustrating and writing sentences about their weather wishes. For example, "Larry wishes it would rain his favorite books." "Kenya wishes the wind would blow birthday cakes." Combine the pages and create a cover with the children's own silly title, such as "Cloudy With a Chance of Soccer Balls."

Book Activity

Another wonderful weather book is *A Snowy Day,* by Ezra Jack Keats (Puffin, 1976). After reading the book, invite the children to share their impressions of the story. Encourage the class to create a snowy-day mural. Have them paint big snowy hills on light blue mural paper. On separate sheets of paper, invite the children to draw themselves wearing red snowsuits. Ask students to cut out their drawings and glue them to the snowy hills in the mural.

Pocket Chart

Copy this weather rhyme onto oaktag sentence strips.

<u>Windy</u> weather is here today.
We'll <u>fly a kite</u> and shout hooray!
For windy weather is here today.

Brainstorm other types of weather and weather-related activities to substitute for the underlined words in the rhyme. For example, sunny weather and swing on swings; rainy weather and splash in puddles; snowy weather and build a snowman.

Hanging Poem Chart

Write the weather poem (on page 85) on your hanging chart. Read it with the class, running your finger under each word. Assign lines to groups of students to recite as a choral reading. Invite children to illustrate the poem, too.

Wonderful weather, what does it do?
It rains on gardens, and on me and you.
Wonderful weather, what does it do?
It shines on beaches, and on me and you.
Wonderful weather, what does it do?
It blows on sailboats, and on me and you.
Wonderful weather, what does it do?
It snows on ski slopes, and on me and you.
Wonderful weather, what does it do?
It makes the world beautiful for me and you!

Writing Journal

Open an umbrella indoors in a clear, safe place, and spin it for children to see. Ask them what images come to mind when they see the umbrella—rainy days, sunny days, at the beach, and so on. Ask children to choose an umbrella occasion and to draw it in their writing journals. Encourage them to write a sentence or two to describe the umbrella scene.

Writing Table

On your writing table arrange shoes that represent different types of weather, such as sandals, flip-flops, snow boots, sneakers, and galoshes. Have children choose a shoe or boot and trace around its shape. Then have them write a sentence about the shoe and the weather it is worn in. For example, "Sandals are fun in the sun," or, "Winter boots keep our feet warm in the snow."

Math Activities

Graphing

Invite children to keep track of the weather in your community for one month. On chart paper, create a large graph on which children can mark the daily temperatures. On the vertical axis, write the numbers for degrees, and on the horizontal axis, write the numbers for the days. Have children mark a dot for each day and its temperature. After a month, connect the dots to see the weather pattern. Is the temperature slowly going up or down? Was there an unusually hot or cold day?

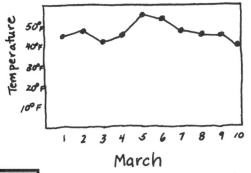

Counting

Which forms of weather have children experienced? Start a chart for children to list their names. Head each column with different weather, such as Fog, Hurricane, Thunderstorm, Rainbow, Tornado, Snow, Blizzard, Hail and Sleet. If children have seen these weather phenomenon, encourage them to sign their names in the appropriate columns. They can sign their names more than once. Count the signatures in each column and write the numbers at the bottom. Which kinds of weather have most children seen?

Problem Solving

Come up with weather-related math problems for children to solve. For example, "4 clouds each have 3 raindrops. How many raindrops are there in all?" Challenge children to write number equations for their weather problems and then solve them. For example, write $4 \times 3 = ?$ or $3 + 3 + 3 + 3 = ?$. Suggest that children also draw the problem to visualize the numbers. (In this case, they would draw 4 clouds with 3 raindrops in each. They could then count all the raindrops.) Write the word problems on index cards and store them in a shoebox decorated with clouds.

Measuring

Divide the class into pairs. Encourage them to cut a cloud shape from white construction paper. Invite children to walk around the room to measure and compare objects with their cloud shapes. Have them write simple sentences to record the comparisons. For example, "The pencil sharpener is smaller than our cloud," or "The fish tank is as long as three clouds."

Patterning

Have students create patterns using rubber stamps of suns, snowflakes, raindrops, and clouds. On strips of paper, have them arrange the stamps in patterns, such as ABBCABBC or any other pattern they design themselves. Suggest that they challenge their classmates to recognize and complete their patterns.

Science Activities

Observation

How much rain falls in your area? Invite children to "collect" rain to find out. Place a plastic bucket outdoors where it won't be disturbed. At about the same time each day, have children measure the amount of water in the pail. Suggest that they record their answer in a bar graph, adding the new amount of water each day. If it rains at the beginning of your observation period, but then doesn't rain for several days, children might actually observe the water level going down. Explain that this happens because the water evaporates into air.

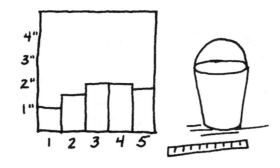

Experiment

Different weather occurs with a combination of hot and cold air and water. Encourage children to experiment to see this for themselves. Pour one inch (2.5 cm) of hot water in a wide-mouthed jar. Place a metal tray of ice cubes on top of the jar. Set the jar in a dark place. Shine a flashlight on the jar and watch for the cloud to appear inside. Tiny raindrops may even begin to fall from the cloud!

Can children figure out why this happened? Explain that when air from the hot water hit the cold air created by the ice-cube tray, it condensed, forming the cloud. As the cloud continued to cool, water drops formed and fell as rain. This is what happens in the atmosphere, too. Hot air and cool air act upon water vapor to create clouds, fog, rain, and even hail and snow!

Investigation

Explain that wind is moving air. Have children work in groups to investigate how wind can move things. Give each group a plastic feather, a sheet of paper, a cotton ball, a toy, a marble, and a metal screw or bolt, and one straw for each group member. Have the children identify the items they think will be easy to move. Record the students' ideas on the chalkboard. Challenge the group members to blow through the straws to move the various objects. Which objects were easy to blow around? Which were not? Check the results against the children's predictions.

Classification

Using index cards, create weather and clothing pictures for children to match. Make sure you have one card for each child. You need to make several suns, raindrops, and snow cards to match with different articles of clothing. For example, create four raindrops to match with a yellow raincoat, a rain hat, galoshes, and an umbrella. Make four suns to match with sunglasses, a bathing suit, a pair of shorts or a T-shirt, and sandals. For snow, make cards with mittens, a wool hat, a heavy coat, and a scarf. Give one card to each child, and challenge them to find the clothing or weather symbol to complete the match. Review the matches, then pass out the cards again to continue the game.

Research

Invite children to further research how weather is formed. Encourage them to explore nonfiction children's books with a weather emphasis. If possible, invite a weather expert to talk about weather with the class, or set up a field trip to a weather station in your area. (Check with a local television news program for ideas.) Invite children to share what they learn by creating weather information posters to display in your science center.

Art Activities

Easel Painting

Invite the class to paint outdoor scenes of sunny days, fall days, or even snowy days. Then fill a spray bottle with diluted blue paint, and spray children's paintings from a distance of about 18 inches (45 cm). Children's paintings will suddenly turn into rainy day scenes!

Ice Prints

Place ice cubes in a metal bowl. Invite children to choose a cube to paint with various colors, then place it on a sheet of white paper. As the ice cube melts, the colors will create a striking pattern. Encourage children to observe their melting masterpieces!

Friends and Hearts Quilt

Learning how precious friends are is an important lesson at any age. This cooperative quilt celebrates the joy of friendship, along with the love of the Valentine's Day season. Heart patches striped with ribbons blend with charming friendship patches. And bright pink bows tie it all up with a cheery valentine border. Good friends warm our hearts and brighten our days, and so will this Friends and Hearts quilt.

Border Patch

Distribute one pink 9" x 9" (22.5 cm x 22.5 cm) patch to each student. Show them how to draw a plus sign in the center, equally dividing the patch into four squares. Have them draw a rectangle at an angle in the center, as shown, then to erase the plus-sign lines inside the rectangle. They've created a bow shape on the patch! Ask children to color in the opposite corners with a red marker or crayon (see example).

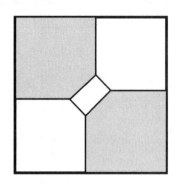

Heart Patch

Create a heart-shaped pattern for children to trace onto pink construction paper and cut out. Have them glue the heart to a 9" x 9" (22.5 cm x 22.5 cm) white quilt patch. Then provide children with red and white ribbons to glue to their hearts. For variation, have children glue the stripes vertically and horizontally.

Glyph Factor

Directions for making glyphs are found on page 6. Ask the children if they have finished writing out their class valentines. Have the children record their answers on their heart patches.

- ◆ If students have written all their class valentines, glue red and white ribbons to their hearts.
- ◆ If students have only written some of their class valentines, glue only red ribbons to their hearts.
- ◆ If students haven't written any of their class valentines, glue only white ribbons to their hearts.

Friend Patch

Encourage children to create two figures out of construction paper, fabric scraps, yarn, wrapping paper, and ribbon to represent two best friends. You might provide children with a paper-doll pattern to make drawing the figures easier. Ask students to glue their paper friends to a pink 9" x 9" (22.5 cm x 22.5 cm) quilt patch.

Literature Connections

Book Activity

Share the book *May I Bring a Friend?*, by Beatrice de Regniers (Simon & Schuster, 1989). If children could bring "friends" to class, who would their friends be? Encourage the class to write its own book about it. Suggest that each student draw a picture of himself or herself with a special friend. Then ask them to write a caption for the picture, for example, "Oscar brought his friend to school. It was a very tall giraffe." Challenge children to make their friends as unique as possible. Create a cover for the book and title it "May We Bring Our Friends to Class?" Then bind the pages together with staples or yarn. Keep the class book in your reading center.

Pocket Chart

Write each line of this poem on a sentence strip to display in a pocket chart. You might at first only show the first four lines. Once children get a feel for the rhyming pattern, place the next three lines in the chart. Hold up the remaining sentence strips, and challenge children to find the rhyming fourth line.

Hearts with ribbons.   *Hearts with candy.*   *Hearts with smiles.*
Hearts with bows.   *Hearts with dots.*   *Hearts with doves.*
Hearts with flowers.   *Hearts with stripes.*   *Hearts with lace.*
Hearts with rows.   *Hearts with spots.*   *Hearts with love.*

Hanging Poem Chart

Write this simple Valentine's Day rhyme on your hanging chart.

Roses are red.
Violets are blue.
This valentine's special.
I made it for you!

Suggest that children copy the rhyme to write in their own Valentine's Day cards to classmates. Or, read the poem several times over the next few days. Each time you read it, place a different student's photo at the end of the last line. Make sure you honor all your students.

Playing with Letters

Play a variation of the game "Hangman" with the class. On the chalkboard, draw nine blanks to represent the nine letters in the word *valentine*. Also draw a heart shape. Can children figure out this mystery word? Encourage them to suggest letters. If a letter is part of the word *valentine*, write it in the proper blank. If not, write the letter inside the heart. After each correct letter, challenge children to guess the mystery word. Continue until the mystery word has been revealed.

For another word game, brainstorm with children all the words they can spell using the letters in *valentine*. Have children work with partners, writing down their words. After a specified time period, invite children to share their words, listing them on the chalkboard in categories of two-letter words, three-letter words, and so on. Here are some to get you started: *an, it, in, at, ten, tin, tan, net, van, vat, vet, lean, vale, line, nine, vane, vein, vine.*

Writing Journal

Valentine's Day is a good time to reflect about not only the people we love, but the things we enjoy doing. Invite children to write about someone or something they particularly like. Suggest that they write simple sentences like, "Alec loves soccer," or "Alicia loves her grandmother." Ask children to illustrate their sentences, too.

Writing Table

Place materials on your writing table for children to make their own Valentine's Day cards, such as patterns for tracing different-size hearts, heart stamps, stickers, wrapping paper with hearts, and so on. Encourage children to fold sheets of paper in half and decorate them with hearts. Ask children to print their own Valentine's Day messages inside or perhaps the poem from the hanging chart activity (page 91).

Math Activities

Graphing

What are children's favorite colors? Cut heart shapes from different colors of construction paper, such as blue, purple, green, yellow, orange, and, of course, red. Glue each heart to the top of a column. Then ask children to sign their names under the colors that are their favorites. Discuss the results. Which color is most popular? How can they tell? Challenge children to count the signatures in each column to confirm the answer.

Estimation

Bring an unopened bag of candy hearts to class. Challenge the children to estimate the number of candies they think are in the bag. Write children's estimates on the chalkboard. As a class, have volunteers help count the candies. Place ten candies at a time in separate cups to help keep track. Whose estimate was closest?

Counting Game

Use your "Concentration" game board (directions on page 6) to play this counting game. Create 20 paper hearts, just the right size to fit in a square of the game board. Tell children to roll a die, then count out that number of hearts and place each on a square. The game ends when all the hearts are on the board. Ask children to count all the hearts.

Sorting

Bring several different packages of Valentine's Day cards to class. Give each student a card, then challenge children to sort their valentines in various ways. For example, by color, by design, or by size. Invite children to swap valentines, and then sort themselves again according to category.

Measuring

Divide the class into small groups. Provide empty heart-shaped candy boxes for each to use as measuring tools. Have students share their findings. For example, "One candy box is smaller than the globe." "My desk is two candy boxes long." Encourage the children to measure their own heights in candy boxes.

Weighing

Have children practice weighing items using a balance scale, math cubes, and boxes of valentines. Encourage students to record their results by completing such sentences as, "1 box of valentines weighs 11 math cubes."

Science Activities

Observation

Remind children that a real human heart looks nothing like a valentine's heart. Provide children with nonfiction science books, and review with them what a human heart looks like. Depending on the age of your students, you might encourage them to research how the human heart works. If possible, share with the class a human-heart model that children can take apart and explore. Suggest that children draw pictures of human hearts in their science journals.

Research

Stress with children that because our hearts pump blood and oxygen through our bodies, it is important to keep them healthy. We can accomplish this by eating healthy foods and getting plenty of exercise. Ask your physical education teacher to also talk with the class about maintaining a healthy lifestyle, perhaps teaching the children an age-appropriate aerobics routine.

Experiment

Invite a health professional from a local hospital, clinic, or doctor's office to come and talk to the children about their hearts. Ask the person to provide several stethoscopes for the children to listen to their classmates' hearts at work.

Investigation

Challenge pairs of students to learn one interesting fact about the heart to share with the class. Start a chart of "Heart Facts." Each time the children learn something new, encourage them to list it on the chart.

Cooking Healthy Foods

Bring in a variety of unopened or empty food containers, such as cereal boxes and canned fruit and vegetables. Then help children read the nutrition labels on the products. Remind children that nutritionists suggest we should eat foods low in fat to keep our hearts healthy. After reviewing and making conclusions about the various foods, eat a healthy snack with the class, such as yogurt dip and vegetables, or frozen grapes. Review the food pyramid to guide children in their eating habits.

Class Visitor—Doctor or Nutritionist

Invite a doctor or nutritionist to talk to your class about healthy eating and exercise habits. Suggest that the visitor first explain how our bodies work, then relate why eating healthy and getting plenty of exercise is important. Encourage children to ask questions. After the visit, have children create information posters to share the healthy facts they learned. Have the class dictate a thank-you letter to send to your special visitor.

Art Activities

Clay Hearts

Invite children to mold valentine hearts from clay. Provide them with a variety of beads, glitter, stickers, fabric scraps, and other art materials. Show them how to press the items into the clay to decorate their hearts. Allow the hearts to dry before handling. Encourage children to present their hearts to family members on Valentine's Day.

Heart Flowers

Have children cut out six small hearts from red and pink paper, along with a medium-sized circle from yellow paper. Show children how to glue the hearts around the circle to resemble flower petals. Invite children to write a special valentines message in the center circle. Then glue on a green chenille stem. Encourage children to make as many heart flowers as they wish for a full Valentine's Day bouquet. Invite children to pass out their flowers to family members, person's in the community, or workers at school, such as the school librarian, the nurse, the principal, the music teacher, cafeteria workers, and so on.

Tooth Fairy Tales Quilt

As you teach the children the importance of good dental hygiene, you can celebrate with them the excitement of losing their baby teeth. Students are encouraged to draw self-portraits that show how many teeth they have lost so far. Whimsical tooth fairies fly about. And border patches represent lost teeth. It's as if the tooth fairy has waved her tiny wand over your pearly white cooperative quilt!

Border Patch

Provide each student with a 9" x 9" (22.5 cm x 22.5 cm) blue quilt patch and white paper. Ask them to cut out a rectangle and two triangles, then arrange them on the patch to resemble a tooth, gluing the pieces in place (see illustration).

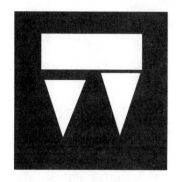

Tooth Fairy Patch

Invite children to create tooth fairies on 9" x 9" (22.5 cm x 22.5 cm) white squares of construction paper. Provide children with an assortment of art materials, such as pastel construction paper for her dress, glitter for her wand, yarn for her hair, and tissue paper for her wings. Help each child assemble his or her tooth fairy on the quilt patch, and when satisfied, glue her in place.

Glyph Factor

Directions for making glyphs are found on page 6. Ask the children if they have lost any teeth yet. Have the children record their answers on their tooth fairy patches.

◆ If students have lost a tooth, suggest that they make the tooth fairy's wand with gold glitter.

◆ If students have not yet lost a tooth, make the tooth fairy's wand with silver glitter.

Missing-Tooth Patch

Ask students to draw self-portraits showing how many teeth they've lost. Have children cut out circles from appropriate skin-tone colored construction paper. Have them draw their mouths as wide toothy grins, leaving gaps for the teeth they have lost. If a child hasn't lost any teeth yet, have that child draw a big toothy smile showing all his or her teeth. Encourage children to draw other facial features, too. Have students glue their smiling faces to 9" x 9" (22.5 cm x 22.5 cm) light blue construction-paper patches. As a finishing touch, suggest that they glue on torn-paper hair. Make sure children write their names on their patches.

Literature Connections

Book Activity

If children aren't already familiar with author Marc Brown's lovable character Arthur, introduce them to him by reading the book *Arthur's Tooth* (Little, Brown, 1985). Afterward, talk with children about the parts of the story they liked best. Encourage them to tell about their own tooth-losing experiences. Or, ask students who have yet lost a tooth to share how they feel about it. Are they anxious? Excited? Perhaps even a little scared?

Pocket Chart

Copy this simple rhyme on sentence strips for your pocket chart. Each time a student is about to lose a tooth, replace his or her name on the sentence strip. Keep track of the children whose names appear in the rhyme, making sure everyone eventually gets a turn. Children will enjoy hearing their names in the rhyme.

Timmy's tooth was loose…
  Where did it go?
Timmy lost his tooth!
  It left a hole!

Hanging Poem Chart

Share this loose-tooth poem with the class by writing it on your hanging chart.

Once I had a tooth,
That wiggled to and fro.
I pulled it with a string
To make it go, go, go.
I hid that little tooth
Under my pillow white.
And the fairy left some money,
That very same night.

Class Book

Share the book *Tooth Fairy*, by Audrey Wood (Childs Play, 1996). What do children think the tooth fairy really does with all the teeth she collects? Encourage children to create a class book to share their ideas. Suggest that they each write a simple sentence, such as, "Kate thinks the tooth fairy gives the teeth to a baby." Invite children to illustrate their sentences. Ask volunteers to make a book cover. Then gather the pages together and staple. Read the class book during your next reading time.

Song

If you have the Raffi collection *Singable Songs for the Very Young* (Shoreline, 1976), play the song "Brush Your Teeth." Once children become familiar with the melody and words, encourage them to sing along with Raffi. For fun, you might ask students to bring in a toothbrush from home to use while singing the song.

Writing Journal

Place a toothbrush in your Feely Box (see instructions on page 7). Can children tell what it is? Invite children to write a description of the item in their journals, guessing its identity and drawing pictures of it, too. Once the toothbrush has been revealed, ask students to write one more sentence explaining why toothbrushes are important.

Writing Table

Ask children how much money they would like to receive for their baby teeth. Provide coin rubber stamps, ink pads, and blank books at the writing table. Encourage children to stamp the pages to show the amount of money they'd like to receive for a loose tooth. Invite each child to write a few sentences explaining what they would buy with this money.

Math Activities

Graphing

What is the most common number of teeth children have lost? Start a horizontal bar graph to find out. Some children might feel self-conscious about the number of teeth they have or haven't lost compared to their classmates. Invite children to take a "silent" vote, writing the numbers on slips of paper. For each vote, draw a tooth shape. Help children read the bar graph to determine how many teeth most children have lost.

Estimation

Place pennies in your estimation jar and show it to the class. Suggest that the tooth fairy is giving out one penny for each tooth she collects. How many pennies does she have? Encourage children to estimate the number of pennies in the jar. Invite children to write their guesses on self-stick notes and place them on the jar. Ask volunteers to help you count the pennies, placing them in stacks of five or ten. How many pennies does the tooth fairy have? Which student's estimate was closest?

Counting

How many teeth does the average mouth have? Display for children a "map" of the mouth, pointing out the three different types of teeth—incisors, canines, and molars. Pass out smaller versions of the mouth map for children to study more closely. Ask the children how many molars they see. How many canines? How many incisors? How many teeth does an average mouth have in all? (A full set of teeth for an adult is 32—16 on the top and 16 on the bottom.)

Brushing Chart

Brushing your teeth is very important for keeping not only your teeth strong and healthy, but your gums as well. Encourage children to keep track of how often they brush their teeth each day. Send home a chart for students to record brushing times. Suggest that children write down the time, along with a little note about the brushing experience. For example, "Bedtime" or "After dinner." Have children record their teeth-brushing schedule for one to two weeks. They might be surprised to see how their brushing improves!

Problem Solving

Present math equations based on losing and growing new teeth. For example, "Last year Julio had 20 baby teeth. He lost 3. How many baby teeth does he still have?" Or, "Lucy has 16 teeth, but 2 new ones are growing in. How many will she have altogether?" Challenge children to write the math equations ($20 - 3 =$; $16 + 2 =$), and then to solve them. If possible, have tooth-shaped manipulatives on hand for children to count out, add, and subtract.

Science Activities

Experiment

Remind children of the three kinds of teeth they saw on the mouth "map" during your math counting activity (page 100)—incisors, molars, and canines. Why do children think they have different kinds of teeth? Invite them to try this simple experiment to find out. Pass out apple slices to students, and ask them to take one bite. Which teeth do they use? Do they use their molars? No, they use their front teeth, or incisors. These teeth are used for cutting food. Our canines are used in a similar way—to tear food. Ask children to continue chewing. Which teeth are being used this time? Now it's the molars. Their job is to grind the food into smaller pieces that can be swallowed and digested. Conclude that our teeth are arranged in a perfect way to process the foods we eat.

Experiment

Try this dramatic demonstration to show children the importance of brushing their teeth. Prepare by gluing small white tiles (about 1-inch square, or 2.5 cm) to a piece of wood. Place the tiles close together to resemble teeth. Make several boards of tiles for children to experiment with in groups. Instruct children to stain the tiles with mustard, coffee, grape juice, and so on, letting the stains dry over several hours. Then encourage children to clean the tiles first with toothbrushes and water, then with toothbrushes, toothpaste, and water. Which combination worked best? Discuss the proper brushing techniques for healthy teeth and gums.

Investigation

Read the book *Berenstain Bears Visit the Dentist,* by Stan and Jan Berenstain (Random Books for Young Readers, 1981). Try to arrange a visit to a local dentist's office. Many children have probably already been to the dentist. This time, invite the dentist to explain all his or her tools and how the tools help keep our teeth clean. Invite children to ask questions, easing their fears about their next dentist appointment. After the visit to the dentist's office, write a class thank-you letter to the dentist for showing them the importance of healthy teeth and gums.

Class Visitor—Dental Hygienist

Encourage a dental hygienist to talk to your class about proper dental hygiene. As a class, prepare a list of questions that the children would like to ask the dental hygienist. Suggest to your tooth expert that she or he describe the process of cleaning teeth. Then have him or her explain why brushing and flossing are so important to healthy teeth and gums. Encourage the dental hygienist to list foods that are harmful to teeth, such as eating too much candy and drinking too much carbonated soda. After the visit, ask students to write thank-you letters describing any new healthy habits they now practice because of the dental hygienist's visit.

Art Activities

Easel Paintings

Set up easels, and encourage children to paint portraits of the tooth fairy visiting them in their own homes while they sleep. Display the paintings for several days, then let children take them home to share with their families.

Toothbrush Creations

Of course, children know that they can paint with paintbrushes. But what about a toothbrush? Invite the children to have fun experimenting with old toothbrushes and paints to see the interesting designs they can create. Encourage students to give their paintings titles and then share them with the class.

Tooth People

Invite each child to cut out a large tooth shape from white construction paper. Encourage them to personalize the teeth by drawing facial features and gluing on construction paper details to make tooth people. Ask children to write healthy tooth tips on their tooth people. Display the tooth people on a bulletin board to help review proper dental hygiene.

Toot! Honk! Zoom! Quilt

Zoom your way into transportation by inviting students to create their favorite ways to travel. Children will mount their vehicles on patches with tire-track backgrounds. The traffic-signal patch reviews when it is time to stop, slow down, and go. And the geometric border adds the finishing touch to your convoy. Big and powerful, fast and noisy, things that go fascinate children of all ages!

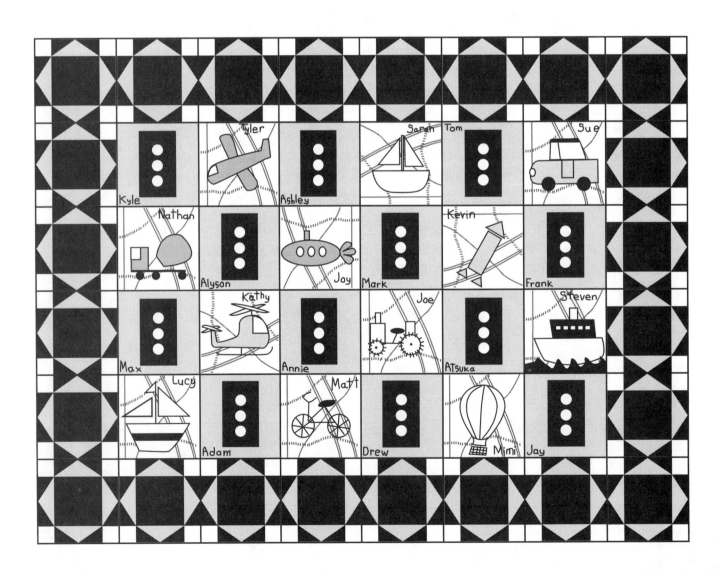

Border Patch

Give each student a 9" x 9" (22.5 cm x 22.5 cm) black square of construction paper. Help them measure four yellow 2" x 2" (5 cm x 5 cm) squares and four red 5" x 3 1/4" x 3 1/4" (12.5 cm x 8 cm x 8 cm) triangles. Depending on the age of your students, provide these shapes yourself. Help students arrange the shapes on the black quilt patch as shown in the illustration.

Vehicle Patch

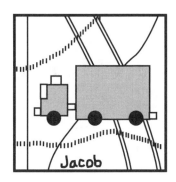

Give each student a 9" x 9" (22.5 cm x 22.5 cm) yellow quilt patch. Working in groups, have them paint tire tracks on their patches. Have the children place their patches in a shoebox lid, then dip the tires of a toy car or truck in black paint. Show them how to roll the vehicle along the patch, leaving tire tracks behind. Then ask children to create a vehicle on another piece of construction paper, cut it out, and then glue it to the patch.

Glyph Factor

Directions for making glyphs are found on page 6. Ask the children how they get to school. Have the children record their answers on their transportation patches.

- ◆ If students ride a bus to school, make a land vehicle.
- ◆ If students walk to school, make a water vehicle.
- ◆ If students ride in a car to school, make an air vehicle.

Traffic-Signal Patch

Help children make traffic-signal patches. Measure and cut out a 4" x 6" (10 cm x 15 cm) black rectangle. Provide scraps of red, yellow, and green construction paper. Cut a circle from each color. Glue the circles in the order of a traffic light on the black rectangle—red on top, yellow in the middle, and green on the bottom. Have students glue the completed traffic signal to a 9" x 9" (22.5 cm x 22.5 cm) red quilt patch.

Literature Connections

Book Activity

Review and sing the traditional song "The Wheels on the Bus." Then share with them the book version *Wheels on the Bus,* by Raffi (Crown Books, 1990). After reading the book through once, encourage children to sing it with you for a second reading. To bring the book to life, create a "bus" on the classroom floor by marking off a large rectangle with masking tape. Arrange chairs in rows to resemble bus seats, then invite children to "get on the bus!" Read and sing the book again. Encourage children to come up with their own verses.

Pocket Chart

Write the following rhyming lines on sentence strips. Then read the lines with the class. Sing the words to the tune of "Here We Go 'Round the Mulberry Bush."

Walk, walk, walk to school.
Walk to school.
Walk to school.
Walk, walk, walk to school,
In all kinds of weather.

How else might children get to school? Brainstorm verbs with the class, allowing them to be real or silly, such as the words *fly, drive, float, chug*, and *ride.* Conclude with the verse, "Come, come, come to school." Substitute the word *come* on the sentence strip. Suggest that children come up with hand motions for the song, too.

Hanging Poem Chart

Copy this transportation poem on your hanging chart to read with the class. Invite children to illustrate the poem to help with future readings.

I hop in a car with a toot, toot, toot.
I soar in a spaceship with a suit, suit, suit.
I ride on a train with a chug, chug, chug.
I pull on my wagon with a tug, tug, tug.

Class Book

Invite students to make a class book based on the song "The Wheels on the Bus." First, discuss other things that might be on the bus and what they might do. List ideas on the chalkboard. For example: kids might sing, the motor might hum, a dog might bark, the driver might wave, and so on. Encourage children's ideas to be whimsical and fun. Divide the class into pairs. Then have children select an idea to write about and illustrate on a book page. Suggest that while one partner writes the sentence, the other partner illustrates it. Combine all the pages together, then invite students to sing their class book.

Car Game

Ask children if they have ever been on a long car trip. What did they do to pass the time? Suggest some of these games, and practice playing them with the class while taking a neighborhood walk. Explain to the children that they are looking for objects that start with each letter of the alphabet, but they must spot them in order. For example, they can not name a D word unless they've already named words starting with A, B, and C. As you walk around the neighborhood, name such things as apple trees, birds, cars, a dog, an evergreen, and so on all the way to Z.

Another game to play on a long car trip is "License Plate Lookout." Each state has its own license plate design. Challenge the children to find as many license plates from different states as they can. The winner of the game is the child who finds the most license plates from other states. They might even see license plates from Canada and Mexico!

Writing Journal

After sharing a number of transportation books, encourage children to think of ideas for places and ways they would like to travel. Encourage children to write simple sentences in their writing journals about a special trip, such as, "I would like to take a plane to Hawaii." Suggest that children also illustrate their journal entries.

Writing Table

Display blank books and rubber stamps with different vehicles on the writing table. Encourage children to create their own transportation books by stamping each page and writing a simple sentence, such as "I can ride on a bus." Encourage students to draw themselves on the vehicles to make their books complete.

Math Activities

Graphing

What kinds of vehicles have the students traveled in? Create a horizontal bar graph to find out. List different "ways to travel" on chart paper, such as cars, trains, planes, boats, buses, subways, bicycles, and trucks. Write the vehicles down the left side of the chart. Ask students to raise their hands if they have ever traveled in one of these vehicles. Draw smiley faces next to each vehicle, one for each vote. Which mode of transportation have most children experienced? Which is the most uncommon type of transportation? How can they tell?

Estimation

Bring to school, borrow from another class, or invite a student to bring in a carrying case for collecting toy cars. Show the case to the class and suggest that it is a parking garage. How many cars are parked here? Record the children's responses on the chalkboard. Challenge children to come up with estimates, then invite volunteers to help count them. Whose estimate was closest?

Counting

Divide the class into pairs. Provide the children with clipboards, tally sheets, and pencils. Have children draw and label different vehicles down the left side of the paper, such as cars, trucks, buses, vans, bikes, police cars, ambulances, and fire trucks. Then take the class outside and invite them to watch the traffic—at a safe distance. Set a time limit of about 10 minutes. Have children draw a tally mark next to each vehicle they see. After returning to the room, ask partners to count all the marks for a final number, then discuss the results.

"Transportation Concentration" Game

Bring out the "Concentration" game board (instructions on page 6) for students to play "Transportation Concentration." Create ten pairs of matching cards of different vehicles, for example two cars, two trains, two buses, two planes, two boats, two bikes, two hot-air balloons, two trucks, two monorails, two mini-vans. Remind students that they are to take turns turning over two cards. If the cards match, they can keep the pair and play again. If not, they turn the cards back over, and it is the next player's turn. The game continues until all matches are found. The winner is the player with the most pairs.

Problem Solving

Place several different toy vehicles on a table and invite children to figure out how many wheels there are in all. Most cars, of course, have four wheels. But many toy trucks and fire engines have more. Have children count and write down the number of wheels on each vehicle, then add all the numbers together to arrive at a total.

Shape Review

Place a variety of shapes in your math center. Ask students to create vehicles using the shapes. Invite children to glue the shapes together on white paper and then label the different shapes they used.

Measuring

Invite children to use several same-sized toy cars to measure items around the room. Have them line the cars up along the item, and then count how many cars it takes to measure it. Ask children to record their findings in a sentence. For example, "The bookshelf is 23 cars long." "My desk is 14 cars long."

Patterning

Provide children with paint and sponges shaped like vehicles, then challenge them to create different patterns of colors and shapes. List patterns for them to make, such as ABAB, AABAAB, ABCABC, and so on. Invite children to show their patterns to the class. Then challenge them to figure out how to complete the pattern. Or, use the pattern strips as a bulletin-board border.

Science Activities

Experiment

Invite children to experiment with toy vehicles and an inclined plane. You will need a large piece of plywood, about 2' x 3' (60 cm x 90 cm), wooden blocks, a toy vehicle, and a stop watch. Start with the board laying flat on the floor. Have children draw a picture of it. Then place a vehicle on one end. How long does it take the vehicle to move to the other end? (It doesn't move.) How can children make the vehicle move? Have them place a block under one end of the plywood, then release the car at the raised end. Ask children to time the descent of the car and record the time. Encourage them to continue raising the board and recording the times. What conclusions can they draw? Invite children to repeat the experiment with other vehicles, too.

Observation

Vehicles help us get from place to place, and they also help us move objects. Invite children to observe this by moving objects in different ways. Divide the class into four teams. Give each team the same number of blocks, but different ways to move them. Team 1 will carry their blocks by hand. Team 2 will push their blocks in a pie tin. Team 3 will carry their blocks in a purse. And Team 4 will load their blocks into a wagon. Have the teams count the number of trips to move the blocks from one end of the room to the other. Which team had the fewest and easiest trips? (Most likely the wagon.) Ask the children what this experiment tells us about how vehicles help us transport things.

Sorting

Collect a variety of toy vehicles for children to sort. Suggest that they sort the vehicles by land, sea, air, or by how they are used. For example, for work or for play. Ask children to make a chart. Then draw pictures of the vehicles in the appropriate columns.

  © Fearon Teacher Aids FE7947

Investigation

Plan a field trip to a local transportation site, such as an airport, a train station, a taxi dispatch, a ferry depot, or a trucking company. As a class, if possible, arrange for children to go for a ride. Encourage the children to observe how these vehicles operate behind the scenes.

Class Visitor—Transportation Expert

Invite someone in the transportation field to visit the class, such as a pilot, train conductor, truck driver, or sailor. Encourage the person to talk about and compare the different ways people and things travel. Invite children to ask questions, and make sure they send thank-you cards to the visitor.

Art Activities

Easel Paintings

Invite children to paint pictures of their favorite ways to travel. Once the paint has dried, cut out the vehicles and glue them to a large length of butcher paper. Title the class mural, "Toot! Honk! Zoom!" Hang the mural in the hallway for others to enjoy.

Cardboard Car Creations

Create large cardboard cars for children to "drive" around the classroom. Invite children to help paint a large-sized box. Cut out the bottom and the top of the box. Poke four holes in the box and attach large paper plates with brads for wheels. Glue two smaller paper plates to the front for headlights, and plastic-foam food trays to the front and back for license plates. Poke holes in each side of the car and attach a string for the child to wear around his or her neck. Invite children to wear the cars and role-play being drivers and passengers.

Creepy Crawlies Quilt

Your students will be "busy as bees" as they piece together this insect quilt. The stunning border patches suggest brightly colored butterflies in flight. The alternating quilt patches reflect crawling and flying insects. Insects will go from being "creepy crawlies" to creatures of wonder with this cooperative quilt.

Border Patch

Help each child measure and cut out a 1" x 8" (2.5 cm x 20 cm) strip of any color construction paper and a 4 1/2" x 4 1/2" (11.25 cm x 11.25 cm) square of light colored construction paper. Glue the strip diagonally to a 9" x 9" (22.5 cm x 22.5 cm) blue quilt patch. Then cut the light-colored square in half and glue the two triangular pieces to each side of the strip to create butterfly wings (see illustration). Encourage children to decorate their butterfly wings with symmetrical patterns.

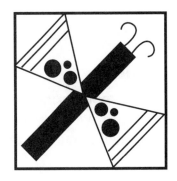

Glyph Factor

Directions for making glyphs are found on page 6. Ask the children about their insect experiences. Have the children record their answers on their butterfly patches.

◆ If students have observed ants going to and from an anthill, paint stripes on the butterfly wings.

◆ If students have ever seen a butterfly sipping nectar from a flower, paint dots on the butterfly wings.

◆ If students have been stung by a bee, paint large spots on the butterfly wings.

Crawling Insect Patch

Give each student a 9" x 9" (22.5 cm x 22.5 cm) square of light blue construction paper and a 9" x 3" (22.5 cm x 7.5 cm) rectangle of green construction paper. Show children how to snip the green paper on the long side to make blades of grass. Glue the grass to the bottom of the square. On another sheet of paper, ask children to draw a crawling insect. Have insect reference books available for children to refer to when choosing their insects. Invite children to cut out the insects and glue them in the grass blades.

Flying Insect Patch

For flying insects, ask students to glue cotton-ball clouds and a yellow paper sun on a 9" x 9" (22.5 cm x 22.5 cm) light blue quilt patch. Encourage students to research insects that fly, such as dragonflies, bees, and house flies. Invite students to draw a flying insect on white paper. Have them cut out the insects and glue them to the sky.

Literature Connections

Book Activity

Read the book *In the Tall, Tall Grass,* by Denise Fleming (H. Holt, 1991). Point out the wonderful illustrations. Invite children to create an insect mural, complete with tall, tall grass. Display the mural in the library with copies of the book.

Pocket Chart

Copy this insect rhyme on sentence strips. Cut apart each verb from the strip, then present children with the first three lines. Challenge them to find the rhyming word to make each verse complete. After reading the poem several times, encourage children to add hand motions, too.

> *Some insects fly.*
> *Some insects crawl.*
> *Some insects jump.*
> *Some insects fall.*
> *Some insects buzz.*
> *Some insects bite.*
> *Some insects dig.*
> *Some insects light.*
> *Some insects sing.*
> *Some insects lay eggs.*
> *Some insects make honey.*
> *But ALL insects have six legs.*

Hanging Poem Chart

Review with children this nursery rhyme by writing it on your hanging chart.

> *Ladybug, ladybug,*
> *Fly away home.*
> *Your house is on fire.*
> *Your children are gone.*

Confirm that ladybugs are, indeed, insects. They are part of the beetle family. Invite children to decorate paper airplanes to resemble ladybugs, then toss them around the room as children recite the nursery rhyme.

Spelling Game

Write simple insect names on the blank sides of large index cards. Draw a picture to help identify each insect. Create enough letter cards from small index cards to spell all the insect names.

Give each child one letter card. For example, if one insect card has the word "wasp," you will need the four letter cards *w, a, s,* and *p.* The teacher holds up a card with an insect name written on it. The object of the game is for each child to hold up his or her card if the insect name contains his or her letter. If another student with the same letter card is already holding it up, the other child must wait for a new insect. The game is complete when all the insect names have been spelled. Invite children to line up with their letter cards in correct order to spell the insect name for the class. Collect the cards, shuffle, and pass them out again.

Writing Journal

Check with a local hobby, craft, educational, or toy store for a collection of plastic insects. Place the plastic bugs in your Peek Box. (directions, page 7.) Invite children to identify the insects. Encourage children to write about one of the insects in their writing journals, perhaps sharing an experience or their feelings. Ask children to illustrate their entries, too.

Writing Table

Provide sheets with the following headings: 1 bug, 2 bugs, 3 bugs, 4 bugs, more bugs. Explain that insects have three body parts. Have each child press a finger to an ink pad and then to paper three times to make one insect. Ask children to make as many insects as indicated on the sheet. Suggest that they draw in six legs, wings, antennae, and faces. Have the children write sentences about their insects, too. For example, "One insect sat on a flower. Two insects crawled in the grass."

Math Activities

Graphing

How do children feel about insects? Do they like them? Not like them? Have no opinion? Create a three-column chart to record children's answers. Ask them to sign their names in the appropriate columns. Help children read the graph to determine how the students feel about insects.

Estimation

Place a number of plastic insects in your estimation jar. Ask students to estimate, not how many insects are in the jar, but how many legs. Remind children that insects have six legs, so their estimates should be in multiples of six. Record the estimates on the chalkboard. After everyone has supplied a number, ask students to count the insects. As a class, add up the multiples of six to arrive at the total number of legs. Which student's estimate was correct?

"Guess the Category" Game

Insects have characteristics distinctive from other animals. They have three body parts and six legs. Spiders are not insects, neither are scorpions, tics, centipedes, millipedes, potato bugs, silver fish, or slugs. Can children distinguish insects from other creepy crawlies? Create two circles on the floor with either yarn or chalk, labeling one "Yes" and the other "No." Place pictures or plastic replicas of insects and other assorted creepy crawlies in a bag. Pull out an ant and place it in the "yes" circle. Pull out a spider and place it in the "no" circle. Can children guess the category? Continue sorting the creatures. Review the physical features that make insects unique.

Counting

Set up your "Concentration" game board (directions on page 6) along with 20 ladybug cards or 20 plastic ladybugs. Ask children to pretend that the game board is a ladybug's home. Have children recite the nursery rhyme on your hanging chart (page 114), then roll a die. Have them count out the same number of ladybugs as on the die and place them on the spaces of the game board. Continue until all the ladybugs are "home."

Measuring

Explain that a caterpillar is really a young butterfly or moth. Draw a caterpillar that is exactly one foot in length (30 cm). Divide the caterpillar into 12 one-inch (2.5 cm) body sections. Invite children to use the caterpillar as a ruler. Suggest that they convert their caterpillar measurements into feet and inches (meters and centimeters). For example, "A floor tile is 2 caterpillars long. That means it is 2 feet (60 cm) long. The flag pole is 3 caterpillars and 4 body sections long. That means it is 3 feet, 4 inches (approximately 1 meter) long."

Science Activities

Experiment

Can students locate an anthill without even seeing it? Try this experiment. At the start of the day, go outdoors and place several types of food on the ground (in an area that won't be disturbed by humans), such as pieces of bread, grains of sugar, potato chips, and cookies. In the afternoon, check the foods. Have they attracted ants? Does one food seem to be preferred by the ants? Quietly, have children try to follow one ant to see if they can locate its home.

Observation

Invite children to quietly observe insects in action. Take the class outdoors, asking them to bring along their science journals. Sit in the grass or on a stoop and ask them to watch for insects. Encourage them to write a short sentence in their science journals to describe one of the insects they saw. Have the children draw their insect observations, too.

Investigation

Did children know that a beautiful butterfly starts life as a caterpillar? Invite children to investigate the life cycles of insects. Most insects follow a four-stage metamorphosis—an egg, which hatches a larva, which changes into a pupa, which hatches the adult. In butterflies, the larva is the caterpillar and the pupa is the cocoon or chrysalis. Have children draw life-cycle circles to show what they have learned.

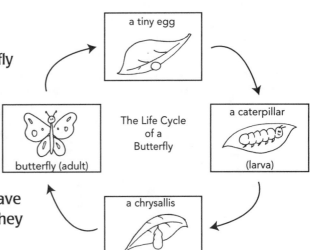

a tiny egg

a caterpillar
(larva)

The Life Cycle
of a
Butterfly

a chrysallis
(pupa)

butterfly (adult)

Class Visitor—Entomologist

Check with a local college or children's museum for a resident entomologist or insect expert. Ask the visitor to bring in insects that children can hold or observe. Encourage children to ask questions. After the visit, have students send thank-you notes to the insect expert, perhaps sharing their favorite parts of the visit.

This quilt explodes with nature's floral fireworks. Big flower patches burst from the border. Gardening-glove patches add children's own individuality as they plant seeds. And tissue-paper blossoms create a three-dimensional effect to bring your gardens to life. This cooperative quilt is a springtime bouquet that will brighten your class in any season.

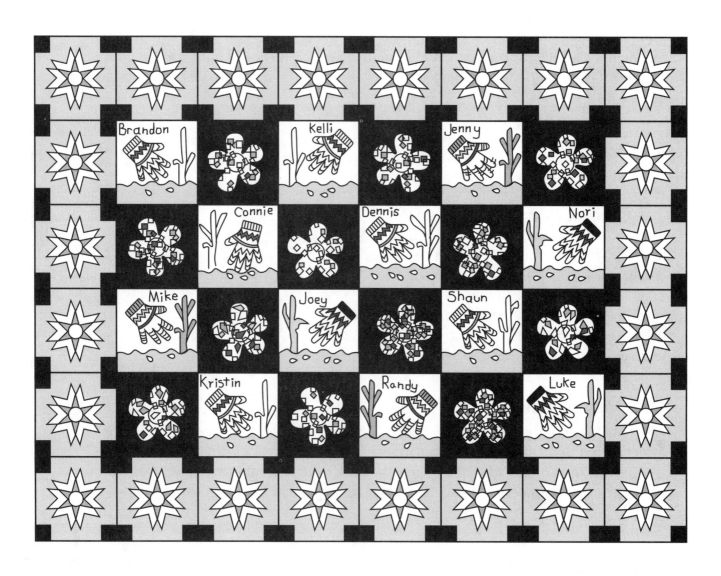

Border Patch

Invite children to create star-shaped flowers on brown 9" x 9" (22.5 cm x 22.5 cm) patches. Help them draw the shapes shown on the border patch. Or, trace the outer shape, and then the inner star shape to create pattern templates. Enlarge the shapes on a photocopier. Pass out the templates for children to trace onto yellow and orange paper. Have them cut out the shapes and then glue them to the center of the patch. For a finishing touch, suggest that children add small squares to the corners of the patches.

Glyph Factor

Directions for making glyphs are found on page 6. Ask the children about their gardening experiences. Have the children record their answers on their flower patches.

- ◆ If students' families have gardens at home, make the flower center red.
- ◆ If students' families do not have gardens at home, make the flower center blue.
- ◆ If students like to garden, make the corner squares blue.
- ◆ If students do not like to garden, make the corner squares red.

Sarah

Gardening-Glove Patch

Invite each student to trace a hand on white paper, color it to resemble a garden glove, and then cut it out. Have children tear brown construction paper into 9" x 3" (22.5 cm x 7.5 cm) strips for the soil. Then tear green construction paper into the shape of a plant. Give each student a 9" x 9" (22.5 cm x 22.5 cm) light blue quilt patch. Arrange the pieces on the quilt patch as shown and glue in place. Finish the patch by drawing in seeds falling from the glove and into the soil.

Flower Patch

Have students draw a circle about 5" (12.5 cm) in diameter on heavy paper, then paint over it with diluted white glue. While the glue is still wet, have students tear colored tissue-paper pieces and stick them to the glue. Allow the tissue paper designs to dry. Cut out flower shapes from the tissue-paper creations. Ask students to glue the flowers to 9" x 9" (22.5 cm x 22.5 cm) patches of dark blue construction paper.

Literature Connections

Book Activity

As a class, read the book *Planting a Rainbow*, by Lois Ehlert (Harcourt Brace, 1988). Discuss the children's own flower-garden experiences. For example, describing special gardens they've seen or sharing times when they've helped family members plant gardens. Pass out small paper flowers in rainbow colors, one for each child. Encourage all the children to arrange themselves into a class rainbow. Review colors of the rainbow—red, orange, yellow, green, blue, indigo, and violet.

Pocket Chart

Write this four-line poem on sentence strips to manipulate in your pocket chart. Substitute strips with children's names and the flower colors—red, orange, yellow, green, blue, indigo, and violet. Invite the child whose name you called to hold up the flower he or she received from the book activity (above). Ask the class to identify the color and place the proper color word in the pocket chart.

Ashley planted red flowers,
In a garden row.
She watered them each day,
So they would grow, grow, grow.

Hanging Poem Chart

Write the poem (on page 121) on your hanging chart. Invite children to say it with you. Give each child a paper flower. Have ten children line up in front of the room holding their different colored paper flowers. For each verse of the poem have a child from the audience come to the front of the room and pick a "flower child." Then both children return to their seats. Continue until all the "flowers" have been picked.

Ten little flowers grow by the grape vine.
_____ picks a red one. Now there are nine.

Nine little flowers grow by the garden gate.
_____ picks a yellow one. Now there are eight.

Eight little flowers grow halfway up to heaven.
_____ picks a purple one. Now there are seven.

Seven little flowers grow by the pile of sticks.
_____ picks an orange one. Now there are six.

Six little flowers grow by the beehive.
_____ picks a blue one. Now there are five.

Five little flowers grow by my back door.
_____ picks a red one. Now there are four.

Four little flowers grow under my tree.
_____ picks a yellow one. Now there are three.

Three little flowers grow in the morning dew.
_____ picks a purple one. Now there are two.

Two little flowers grow under the sun.
_____ picks an orange one. Now there is one.

One little flower grows as pretty as can be.
_____ picks the last one. Now there's none for me!

Word-Match Game

Bring out the "Concentration" game (instructions on page 6) to play this matching game. Create ten pairs of matching cards. One card will be a picture and the matching card will have words. For example, one child might have a picture of a red flower. Another child has a card with the words *red flower*. The object is for each student to find his or her match by reading the cards and studying the pictures. You can make other sets of cards for numbers (three flowers), patterns (striped flower), shapes (circle flower), or a combination (two pink-striped circle flowers). Invite children to change cards for another round of play.

red flowers

white flower

yellow flower

Writing Journal

To prompt children's writing, place a variety of seeds in the Feely Box (directions on page 7) for children to examine through their sense of touch. Invite children to jot down ideas in their writing journals about something fantastic the seeds might grow, such as Jack's magic beanstalk, a jumbo fruit or vegetable, an amazing flower, and so on. Encourage children's imaginations to grow as they draw pictures of their plants, too.

Math Activities

Graphing

Invite each child to bring one flower to class. Create a graph to record the flowers children brought in. You might record their flowers by type (carnation, mum, rose, tulip) or by color. Which color or type did most children bring in?

Estimation

Divide the class into small groups and hand out one packet of flower seeds to each group. Challenge each group member to estimate the number of seeds in the packet. Then write his or her estimate on a sheet of paper.

Problem Solving

Imagine that each child is a flower, and he or she has four petals. How many petals does the entire class have? Ask children to each cut out four petal shapes from paper, then collect all the petals. Ask children to count the petals by arranging them into piles of ten. Count the piles and the leftover petals to arrive at the total.

Counting

Encourage children to put together flower bouquets with this counting activity. Have each child tape a flower shape to a craft stick. Divide the class into small groups. Have group members pose problems, such as, "Sally planted 5 flowers. Bernard planted 2 flowers. How many flowers will be in our bouquet?" Encourage group members to add the numbers together, then count all the flowers to arrive at the correct answer. Have them also write out the equations. $(5 + 2 = 7)$

Measuring

Have children practice their measuring skills by taking a nature walk outdoors. Supply pairs of children with rulers or yardsticks to measure various flowers and plants. Have the children record the measurements in their journals. For example, "A stalk of grass is 2 inches (5 cm) tall." "A tulip is 5 inches (12.5 cm) tall." Back in class, invite children to share and compare their measurements. Which plants were tallest? Shortest?

Science Activities

Experiment

Invite groups of students to plant sunflower seeds in different substances. Give one group a cup of potting soil, another a cup of sand, another a cup of cotton balls, another a cup of shredded paper, and so on. Encourage the children to predict the substance where the seeds will grow the best. To keep the experiment consistent, make sure the groups give each cup of seeds the same amount of water. Invite children to measure the plants' growth, drawing the results in their science journals.

Identification

Create flower-and-seed cards for children to identify. Tape some seeds to one side of an index card. Tape the empty seed packet to the other side of the cards to identify the flowers. Working in pairs, challenge children to study the seeds and guess which flower will grow from them. The more children practice, the easier it will become to identify the seeds.

Tactile Table

Spread newspaper across your tactile table and fill it with potting soil. Supply children with small scoops, and invite them to explore the soil. Encourage children to view the soil through magnifying glasses to see the small bits of material it is made from. Explain that soil is a combination of broken rocks and decaying plant and animal matter, which provides food for growing plants. If possible, place your tactile table outdoors to reduce the amount of soil spillage inside.

Class Visitor—Botanist

Explain that a botanist is a scientist who studies plants. Invite a botanist or another plant expert, such as a flower-shop worker or a nursery owner, to talk with the class about flowers. Create a list of questions children would like answered, and encourage your visitor to bring in samples of plants for children to explore firsthand. Have children send cards decorated with flowers to thank the flower expert for the visit.

Art Activities

Press-Flower Bookmarks

If children have brought in flowers for any of the activities, encourage them to save the flowers by creating bookmarks. Cut rectangular bookmark shapes from wax paper. Place the flower or petals of the flower between two wax-paper rectangles, waxy sides together. Then place a light cloth over the bookmarks and lightly iron the paper until the wax melts and the halves stick together. Let children use the bookmarks or give them as gifts.

Three-Dimensional Flowers

Help children fold a sheet of 12" x 18" (30 cm x 45 cm) colored construction paper in half, lengthwise. Then fold it lengthwise in half again. Unfold the paper once, so you have a half sheet. Show the children how to make cuts along the entire length of paper from the fold to the crease. Then fold paper as in Figure 2. Bring the two uncut ends of the paper together and overlap them to make a circle. Then staple the ends so it looks like a wreath. Staple or glue construction-paper stems and leaves to make bright big three-dimensional flowers. Display the flowers in a bulletin-board garden.

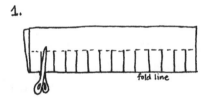

Tell Me a Story Quilt

Throughout time, telling stories has been a way to not only entertain, but to pass down information, cultural lore, and history. Students depict a favorite folktale in quilt fashion by retelling the story of "The Three Little Pigs." The quilt is bordered by patches that reflect the colors of the three pigs' houses—straw, sticks, and bricks. The text patches help tell the story. And the illustration patches add charm and continuity. Display the quilt as a reading treat for the entire school. Be sure to use the basic quilt format to illustrate other stories children enjoy.

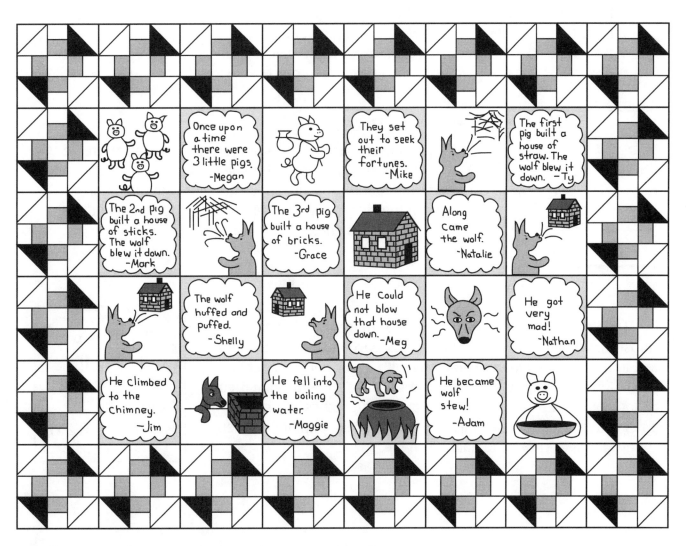

Border Patch

Give each student yellow, brown, and red construction paper. Cut out the following shapes yourself, or have children do it to practice math skills. Ask students to measure and cut out four 3" x 1" (7.5 cm x 2.5 cm) rectangles from red paper, one 3" x 3" (7.5 cm x 7.5 cm) square from yellow paper, and one 3" x 3" (7.5 cm x 7.5 cm) square from brown paper. Have them cut the squares in half from corner to corner to create four triangles. Then help children arrange the pieces on a 9" x 9" (22.5 cm x 22.5 cm) patch. The color for the background patch is determined by the glyph factor (see below).

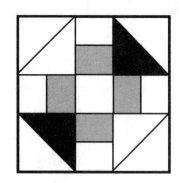

Glyph Factor

Directions for making glyphs are found on page 6. Ask the children about their character in the story "The Three Little Pigs." Have the children record their answers on their border patches.

- ◆ If students like the "straw" pig best, use a light blue patch.
- ◆ If students like the "stick" pig best, use a pink patch.
- ◆ If students like the "brick" pig best, use a white patch.
- ◆ If students like the wolf best, use a pale green patch.

Story-Scene Patch

Assign various parts of the story for each child to re-create on a 9" x 9" (22.5 cm x 22.5 cm) light blue quilt patch. Help them tear construction-paper scraps into shapes to illustrate the different scenes from the story. Help children arrange the pieces and then glue them to their patches.

Text Patch

Help children cut balloon shapes like those used in comic strips from white construction paper. Ask each child to write story text in his or her balloon to go along with his or her story-scene patch. Remind them to sign their names. Have students glue their balloons to 9" x 9" (22.5 cm x 22.5 cm) pink patches. If a computer is available, invite children to type the text, print it out, then cut around it to create the balloon shape.

Literature Connections

Book Activity

Many wonderful adaptations have been published of "The Three Little Pigs." Share the various books with the class, discussing their similarities and differences. Encourage children to vote on their favorites. Here are some to get you started: *The Three Little Pigs* by James Marshall (Dial, 1989); *The True Story of the Three Little Pigs by a Wolf* by Jon Scieszka (Viking, 1989), and *The Fourth Little Pig* by Teresa Celsi (Raintree Steck Vaughn, 1993).

Pocket Chart

Share this rhyme by writing the lines on sentence strips to display in the pocket chart. Invite children to come up with hand motions for the rhyme to make it an interactive experience.

Five little piggies rolling in the dirt.
One ran away. He was hurt.

Four little piggies rolling in the mud.
One ran away. His name was Bud.

Three little piggies rolling in the hay.
One ran away. He wanted to play.

Two little piggies rolling in the rain.
One ran away. He had a pain.

One little piggy rolling in the sun.
He ran away. Now there were none.

Hanging Poem Chart

Review this popular nursery rhyme by copying it onto your hanging chart. Invite children to share the ways they've recited the rhyme, including any hand motions.

This little piggy went to market.
This little piggy stayed home.
This little piggy had roast beef.
This little piggy had none.
And this little piggy cried, "Wee!" all the way home.

Class Book—Dream Houses

Discuss how each of the three little pigs built a house that he thought was best for him. If students could build a dream house, which materials would they use? Encourage their ideas to be silly and imaginative. For example, their houses could be built with cookies, or computer games, books, or videos. Have children write simple sentences, such as "Adam's house would be made from computer games." Then invite the children to draw their houses. Encourage volunteers to create a book cover with the title, "Our Dream Houses." Then staple the pages together and read the book with the class.

Writing Journal

Place the materials the three little pigs used for constructing their houses—some straw, a stick, and part of a brick in your Feely Box (see page 7). You might include all three, or just one. Relying on the children's sense of touch, encourage them to describe the materials in their writing journals. Challenge them to speculate why one building material might have been better than the other.

Put on a Play

Invite your class to act out the story of "The Three Little Pigs," either following the traditional tale, or perhaps one of the modern retellings you shared earlier. Assign children to groups, such as set builders (to paint murals of the different houses), costume designers (to create masks from paper grocery bags), sound-effects engineers (to record music and the sound of houses crashing and wind blowing), playwrights (to write the basic dialogue or words for a narrator to speak), and actors and actresses. Set aside time each day for children to work on the play. Then hold rehearsals. When children feel comfortable, encourage them to share their performance with another class or family members.

Math Activities

Problem Solving

Incorporate the three little pigs into math problems for children to solve. For example, pretend with the class that the three pigs have been invited to a party. They can each bring one guest. If they all drove together in the same car, how many little pigs would there be?

Help children write the equation 3 x 2 =, then arrive at the answer. Or, suggest that the little pig in the brick house decided to have a party to celebrate his victory over the wolf. The "straw" pig brought 5 guests. The "stick" pig brought 4 guests. The "brick" pig invited 6 friends of his own. How many pigs were there in all? Remind children not to forget the three pigs themselves! (3 + 4 + 5 + 6 = 18) Encourage children to come up with their own fun pig problems for classmates to solve.

Counting

Use your "Concentration" game board (directions on page 6) for this counting game. Gather together 20 plastic pigs. Or, make pig cards to place on each space on the game board. You might also use cubes or other manipulatives to represent the pigs. Tell children to roll a die, count out that number of pigs, and place them on the board, one to a square. At the end, they must roll the exact number to place the remaining pigs on the board. Invite children to continue by rolling the die, counting, and taking off that number of pigs.

Measuring

Take children outside to find sticks to use as measuring tools. Make sure the sticks aren't too long or pointy. Have children measure items on the school playground. Working in pairs or small groups, invite one group member to record the measurements, such as "The slide is 8 sticks tall."

Science Activities

Observation

Discuss how the three little pigs built their homes from three different materials. Which materials can children recognize in buildings around your school? Take the class on a neighborhood walk to see the different constructions. Children might see homes with brick, wood, or aluminum-siding fronts. Others might have clay or stucco exteriors. If you live in a city, point out bricks versus concrete blocks, as well as differences in shape. Back in class, invite children to write about and draw the homes they observed in their science journals.

Experiment

Set up a table with a pile of straw (you might also use dried grass), a pile of sticks, and a pile of bricks. Encourage the children to predict which material will most easily blow away. Record the children's predictions on the chalkboard. Aim a fan directly at the straw pile, and have children recite, "Then I'll huff, and I'll puff, and I'll blow your house in!" Turn on the fan to see what happens (keep children away from the fan). Repeat with the other two piles. Children should notice that the straw blows right off. The sticks give a bit more resistance. But the bricks don't budge at all. After this experiment, which material would children choose to build their own houses?

Investigation

If possible, take the class on a field trip to a construction site where new homes are being built. Before the trip, go over safety procedures with the class. At the site, have children notice the inner structure, comparing it to a skeleton, along with the foundation. Also point out all the people working to build the house. Invite children to ask questions of the construction site foreperson. Back in class, have children draw before-and-after pictures to show what their own homes might have looked like as they were being built. Encourage children to send thank-you notes to the crew of the construction site for allowing them to visit.

Tactile Table

Place sticks, straw, and bricks on your tactile table for children to feel and manipulate. If materials and time allow, you might let children try to build small homes using each of the materials. Have them share their homes with classmates, then ask them to disassemble their structures so others can use the materials, too.

Class Visitor—Architect or Builder

Check with children to see if any parents are architects, builders, or construction workers who might like to talk to the class. Encourage the visitor to explain how houses are designed and built, including his or her own contribution. Have children realize that building a home is a cooperative endeavor that applies the skills of many talented people. Encourage children to dictate a thank-you note to send to the visitor.

Art Activities

Easel Painting

Share the book *A Treeful of Pigs,* by Arnold Lobel (Greenwillow, 1979). Point out the humorous drawings. Then set up easels and encourage children to paint their own large, fanciful pigs. As children work, create a large tree on a classroom wall or bulletin board for children to display their artwork.

Paper-Plate Pigs

Pass out paper plates and invite children to paint them pink. Encourage them to cut out ears, a snout, eyes, and a mouth, and glue or tape them to the plate. Tape a craft stick to the bottom of the plate as a handle. Use the paper-plate pigs as masks or puppets. Have children hold up the pigs as you recite the rhymes or read the stories.

Home Dioramas

Ask children to bring in shoeboxes to create dioramas of the three pigs' homes. (Have shoeboxes on hand for students who forget.) Encourage children to choose one pig and design a home with a straw, stick, or brick motif. Supply children with art materials, such as fabric, toothpicks, craft sticks, and construction paper. Invite children to share their finished products with the class.

A pond is a small world with plenty of action. And so is this cooperative "Pondmania" quilt. Little green frogs leap across the patches, while fish swim playfully around the lily-pad border. Invite children and viewers to "leap" in and learn what life in a pond is all about.

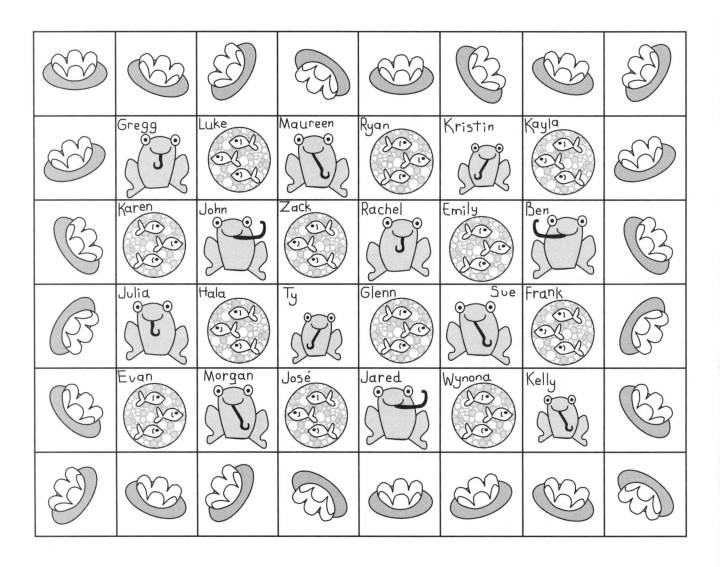

Border Patch

Invite children to create a lily-pad border on 9" x 9" (22.5 cm x 22.5 cm) light blue patches. Have each student cut out an oval lily pad from green construction paper and glue it to his or her patch. Help students make white tissue-paper flowers with yellow centers to glue to the lily pads.

Fish Patch

Invite children to make a water backdrop for this patch. Fill a pie tin with water, mix in dish-washing soap and blue food coloring. Give children straws to blow bubbles in the pie tin. Show them how to lay an 8" x 11" (20 cm x 27.5 cm) white piece of paper onto the bubbles in the pie tin. A circle print will form where the bubbles popped. When the bubble print is dry, have students cut out a big bubble shape and glue it to a 9" x 9" (22.5 cm x 22.5 cm) yellow square. Invite children to use various colors of scrap paper to create fish. Glue fish to the watery patches.

Glyph Factor

Directions for making glyphs are found on page 6. Ask the children about their pond experiences. Have the children record their answers on their fish patches.

- ◆ If students have never been to a pond, make one fish.
- ◆ If students have visited a pond, make two fish.
- ◆ If students have fished at a pond, make three fish.
- ◆ If students have caught frogs at a pond, make four fish.

Frog Patch

Provide children with 9" x 9" (22.5 cm x 22.5 cm) light blue patches and ask them to draw a green frog on it. Refer to Ed Emberley's *Big Green Drawing Book* (Little, 1979) to guide students' frog illustrations. Encourage children to add silly details, such as wiggle eyes and a long red construction-paper tongue.

Alyssa

Literature Connections

Book Activity

To give students a peak at life in a pond, share the book *In the Small, Small Pond* by Denise Fleming (Henry Holt, 1993). Use the book to inspire children's own pond illustrations. Roll out a length of mural paper and lightly draw in the cross section of the land and the pond. Have children fill in the details of the land area. Provide plastic bubble wrap and show children how to dip it into blue paint and press to the pond to make a watery effect. On separate sheets of paper, ask children to paint animals that might live at the pond. When the paintings are dry, have them cut out the animals and glue them to the pond. Display the pond mural in the hall for others to enjoy.

Pocket Chart

As a class, read this counting rhyme. Write the lines on sentence strips to place in your pocket chart. For other verses, substitute the underlined words with other numbers and animals. For example, use 4 and blue fish; 3 and green snake; 2 and black bird; and 1 and yellow duck.

<u>5</u> little frogs were out one day,
At a busy pond to play.
Along came a <u>red bug,</u>
And scared one away.

Hanging Poem Chart

Share this poem by writing it on your hanging chart.

Down by the pond lives a turtle brown.
He is the shyest animal in town.
When he is afraid, he never runs away.
He just pokes in his head and legs,
To stay, stay, stay!

Class Book—At the Pond

Encourage children to contribute a page to a class book about something they would like to do or see at a pond. On same-size sheets of paper, have each student first draw a picture to show the pond activity. Then ask them to write a sentence, such as, "Jimmy watches ducks at the pond," or, "Beth catches frogs at the pond." Ask volunteers to create a cover for the pond book, then bind all the pages together. Read the book to the class.

Writing Table

Supply your writing table with small blank books, about six pages each. Have children copy a simple sentence on each page, such as, "I see ducks at the pond." Make sure children write about a different animal on each page. To illustrate the pages, have children draw in the animals with markers or crayons. Or, provide rubber stamps of fish, ducks, and other pond creatures.

Math Activities

Estimation

Place different amounts of goldfish crackers in three jars. Show children the jars, and challenge them to tell you which jar they think has exactly five scoops. Place the scoop next to the jars for reference. Have children vote on the correct jar. Record the children's responses on the chalkboard. Invite them to test their predictions and scoop out the crackers into another jar or bowl. How many scoops are in each jar? Invite students to enjoy the crackers as a fun pond snack.

Counting Song

If you have available *Singable Songs for the Very Young,* by Raffi (Shoreline MCA, 1976), share with the class the counting song "Five Little Frogs." Encourage children to act out each verse.

"Pondmania Concentration" Game

Create 10 matching pairs of cards of plants and animals children might see at the pond, such as frogs, lily pads, fish, turtles, dragonflies, ducks, cattails, mosquitoes, geese, and snakes. Shuffle the cards and place them face down on your "Concentration" game board (directions on page 6). Ask children to take turns turning over two cards at a time. If the cards match, the player removes them from the board and goes again. If not, the child turns the cards back over, and it is the next student's turn. Play ends when all the matching pairs have been found. The winner is the child with the most matching pairs.

Counting

Read the book *Swimmy,* by Leo Lionni (Knopf, 1973). Encourage children to create their own large fish, filled with smaller fish. On a large sheet of poster board or oaktag, draw the outline of a very large fish. Then provide children with fish-shaped sponges and show them how to dip the sponges into paint to make prints. Help them fill the outline with as many fish as possible, counting all the fish that fit inside.

Science Activities

Research

Although children might think frogs and toads are the same animal, they actually have different characteristics. Read books from the *Frog and Toad* series by Arnold Lobel (HarperCollins, 1970). Help children list the frog and toad differences on a two-column chart. Encourage children to add illustrations, too.

Sequencing

Encourage the children to explore how frogs develop and grow. Go to the library to find books about frogs. Point out the various life stages—from egg to tadpole to changing frog to adult. Pass out a 6" x 12" (15 cm x 30 cm) sheet of white paper to each student. Show students how to fold it into fourths and number the sections from 1 to 4. Invite the students to draw a different stage of a frog's life in each box—egg, tadpole, changing frog, and adult frog.

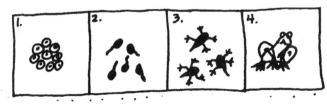

Investigation

Of course, the best way to study a pond is to visit one. If possible, take a field trip to see a pond at a nature center that has knowledgeable guides and children's programs. Suggest that children take along their science journals to draw pictures of the plants and animals they see. Point out that although a pond's surface might seem still and quiet, there are many creatures that live in it, such as fish, insects, frogs, ducks, and other birds. Back in class, have the children write thank-you letters to the nature-center personnel.

Tactile Table

If you have a water table, fill the bottom with sand, then add the water. Provide children with plastic pond plants and animals and encourage them to visit the table to explore what life in a pond might be like.

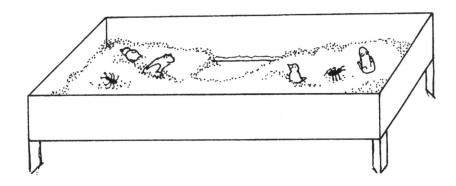

Class Visitor—Pet-Shop Worker

Many pet stores sell animals common to ponds, including frogs, turtles, snakes, and, of course, fish. Invite someone who works at such a pet shop to visit your class to share with children the things these animals need to live. If possible, invite the pet-shop worker to bring animals for children to see. Encourage children to ask questions about the animals, too. Afterward, have children write cards thanking the pet-shop worker for visiting their class.

Art Activities

Rock Pond Animals

Invite children to create pond animals using rocks. Take the class outside to collect rocks, or ask children to bring rocks from home. Encourage children to paint a frog shape on a rock, glue rocks together to make a turtle, paint other rocks to look like fish, and so on. Provide tempera paints, thin paintbrushes, and glue. Allow the rock creatures to dry before handling. Invite children to share their pond animals with their classmates.

Papier-mâché Snakes

Help children create snakes using papier-mâché. First, straighten coat hangers. Then bend the hangers into snake shapes for children to use. Cover the ends of the hangers with masking tape to avoid sharp edges. Help children wrap newspaper and tape around hangers to form snake bodies and heads. Cut cups from egg cartons and tape to the snake's head for eyes. Show children how to cover the snake with papier-mâché newspaper strips. Allow the snakes to dry for several days before handling. Provide library books about snakes for children to see snakes with different kinds of colors, patterns, and designs. Encourage children to paint designs on their snakes.

Farm Friends Quilt

Harness the excitement of visiting a farm with this bold, vivid quilt. The patches capture friendly barnyard animals and sturdy farm buildings, alternating the scenes between night and day. The cow patch border of black and white creates the perfect frame for this farm quilt. This cooperative quilt will inspire children to sing about "Old MacDonald" and other barnyard friends they know.

Border Patch

Divide the class into pairs. Have children work with partners to create the border patches. Give each child a 9" x 9" (22.5 cm x 22.5 cm) white quilt patch. Then give each pair of children a 9" x 9" (22.5 cm x 22.5 cm) black quilt patch. Have one partner cut out wavy splotches from the black paper that resembles the

coloring of a black-and-white dairy cow. Invite one child to glue the black splotch to the white patch, while the other child glues the cutaway part of the black square to the white patch. These patches will not only look like positives and negatives of each other, but they will resemble the coat of a dairy cow.

Barnyard Animal Patch

Encourage children to create daytime farm patches. Provide paper, scissors, crayons, and glue for children to create their favorite barnyard animals. Provide books and other visuals to aid in creating farm scenes. Invite children to glue their animals to a light blue 9" x 9" (22.5 cm x 22.5 cm) patch. Encourage children to add barnyard details with crayons.

Glyph Factor

Directions for making glyphs are found on page 6. Ask the children if they have ever visited a farm. Have the children record their answers on their farm patches.

◆ If students have visited a farm, add a sun to their patches.
◆ If students have not visited a farm, add clouds to their patches.

Barn and Silo Patch

Display pictures of barns and silos, then ask children to draw and cut out farm buildings from construction paper. Have them glue their barnyard buildings to a 9" x 9" (22.5 cm x 22.5 cm) black patch. To make their nighttime farm scenes complete, give children small gold sticker stars to decorate the night sky.

Literature Connections

Book Activity

Your school library probably has quite a collection of books with farm settings. Share some of your favorites with the class. Here is one to get you started—*Barnyard Banter*, by Denise Fleming (Henry Holt, 1994). Encourage children to practice crowing like a rooster, then let them try other farm animal noises, too. Which barnyard animal noise is the class favorite?

Pocket Chart

To practice reading skills, teach children this fun and noisy farm chant. Copy the following lines onto sentence strips to place in the pocket chart.

> *At the farm*
> *I saw a <u>pig.</u>*
> *The <u>pig</u> said, "Oink."*

Replace the underlined words with other farm animals and their sounds. Let children draw animal illustrations to add visual cues.

Hanging Poem Chart

Write the following poem on your hanging chart. Help children read it by pointing to each word as you recite it. Guide students to recognize the repeating words and phrases.

> *Where can you see a pig, pink and round?*
> *At the farm! At the farm!*
> *Where can you see chickens peck at the ground?*
> *At the farm! At the farm!*
> *Where can you see a silo tall?*
> *At the farm! At the farm!*
> *Where can you hear a noisy goose call?*
> *At the farm! At the farm!*

Brainstorm with children other things they might see at the farm, and write their ideas as additional verses for the poem. Your new lines can rhyme, but they don't have to. Recite the complete poem with the class.

Class Book—Come With Me to the Farm

Speculate with children the different things they might see at the farm, including animals, buildings, and plants. Start a list on the chalkboard. Try to have one item for each child in class. Besides animals and buildings you've already discussed, don't forget to include a scarecrow, a corral, a duck pond, a tractor, a plow, and even the farmers themselves. (Make sure you have a male and a female farmer.) Then assign a farm item to each child. Have children draw a picture of their farm items, then write the sentence, "Come with me to a farm and see _____ ," filling in the blank with the item in their illustrations. Encourage students to create a cover with the title, "Come With Me to the Farm," then bind the book and share it with other classes.

Songs

Singing songs is a wonderful way to make children aware of language. On poster board or on your hanging chart, write the words to traditional farm songs that children know. Then invite children to not only sing the song, but read it as well. As children sing the words, be sure to point to them on the chart, making the connection between the written and the oral language. Some songs you might try are the traditional songs "Old MacDonald Had a Farm" or "The Farmer in the Dell." Encourage children to share other farm songs they know, too.

Writing Journal

Place a plastic toy farm animal, such as a horse, a cow, a pig, or a chicken in your Feely Box (directions on page 7). Challenge children to identify the animal, then to write a few words or sentences about it in their journals. Encourage interested students to write a story involving the animal.

Math Activities

Graphing

Create a large chart with four columns on butcher or poster paper. At the top of each column, glue a different picture of a farm animal, such as a cow, a horse, a pig, and a chicken. Other animals you might include are sheep, ducks, goats, roosters, mules, cats, and dogs. Display the chart, and throughout the day, invite children to visit the chart to sign their names under the animals that are their favorites. Tally up the results, and share the favorite barnyard animal at circle time.

Problem Solving

Come up with math problems with a farm theme for children to solve. For example: "If two cows and two chickens live on a farm, how many legs and tails are there in all?" Speculate with children how they can solve the problem, then help them arrive at the answer. Encourage children to come up with their own farm problems to stump their classmates.

Counting Storyboards

Ahead of time, create storyboards by drawing simple farm scenes on poster board or oaktag, then laminating them. One storyboard could show a barn, another a horse corral, another a duck pond, and so on. Present the storyboards to children, along with math manipulatives. Encourage children to come up with addition and subtraction problems as they maneuver the manipulatives on the storyboard. For example, one child might tell the following story: "My dad had six cows in the barn. Four got lost. My dad only had two cows left." Encourage children to be as creative as possible when creating and sharing their math farm stories.

"Farm Animal Concentration" Game

Help children match baby animals with their parents by playing "Farm Animal Concentration." Create pairs of cards of baby and adult animals, labeling the cards with the animal names, too. For example: cow and calf; horse and colt; sheep and lamb; goat and kid; chicken and chick; pig and piglet; goose and gosling; duck and duckling; dog and puppy; cat and kitten. Place the cards face down on your "Concentration" game board (directions on page 6). Then review that the object of the game is to turn over two cards and find a match. If a match is found, the player removes the cards and goes again. If not, it is the next player's turn. The game ends when all the matches have been found. The player with the most matching pairs is the winner.

Patterning

Share the book *Color Farm,* by Lois Ehlert (HarperCollins, 1990). Then invite children to create their own farm animals by cutting out bold, colorful shapes from construction paper and gluing them to black paper. Display children's "color farms" for all to see.

Science Activities

Sorting and Classifying

Most farm animals can be divided into two groups—animals with hooves and birds. Create a two-column chart. Then hold up pictures of farm animals—ones that children have drawn or that you have cut from magazines. Challenge children to identify in which column each animal belongs. Hoofed animals would include horses, cows, pigs, sheep, mules, and goats. Birds would be chickens, ducks, geese, roosters, and turkeys.

Sequencing

Invite children to explore the life cycle of a chicken. Draw each part of the life cycle on an index card, for example, the egg, the egg hatching, the baby chick, and the full-grown chicken. Mix up the cards and challenge children to put them in the proper life-cycle sequence.

Observation

Set up a display that includes different types of pasta, breads, cakes, and cookies. Ask children if they can figure out what all these things have in common. Mention that they all started out in the same place—on a farm! Explain that all these foods are made with flour, which is made from wheat, which is a very important crop for many farmers. As a home-work assignment, encourage children to look at home for items made from flour to share with the class.

Investigation

Locate a nearby farm that invites children for field trips. Encourage children to view the barns, silos, and hen houses, along with the equipment the farmer uses, such as a tractor and a combine. Allow children to ask questions about the farmer's tools, animals, and buildings. Back in class, suggest that children make cards to send to the farmer showing their favorite farm items.

Class Visitor—Veterinarian

Invite a veterinarian to speak to your class about farm animals in particular, but domestic animals in general. Suggest that the vet explain how animal care differs from human care. Encourage the vet to share any of his or her experiences visiting a farm to treat farm animals. Allow children to ask questions during the visit. Afterward, make sure children send thank-you notes to the veterinarian.

Art Activities

Easel Painting

Ask children to close their eyes and to imagine themselves on a farm. Then set up easels, and invite children to paint the farm scenes they imagined. Remind children to include the buildings, farm equipment, and animals that they learned were part of a farm. Let children take their paintings home to share their farm views with their families.

Farm Puppets

Ask children to draw farm animals on construction paper and cut them out. Instruct them to glue the cutouts to a cardboard tube from toilet tissue or paper towels. Then show them how to slip their fingers into  the tubes to use them as puppets. Working in groups, have children come up with short puppet plays involving their farm animals and acting out a day on the farm. Invite the groups to share their puppet plays with the class.

Farm Dioramas

Encourage children to work in groups to create dioramas of farm life. Suggest that they cover a shoebox with red paper to represent a barn. Inside, have them draw stalls with hay, then set up plastic animals to make the barn complete.

Dairy Delights Quilt

Ice cream is a treat that can not only be nutritious, but that most children enjoy. Encourage children to express just how much they like ice cream by creating this cooperative quilt. Pastel pinwheel border patches surround a blanket of berries and creamy scoops. Fruit-and-nut patches convey the healthy foods ice cream is made with. And ice-cream cone patches finish the treat, right down to the last sweet bite. This quilt is sure to dish out scoopfuls of learning.

Border Patch

Help children make a pinwheel shape. Each piece in the diagram measures 3" x 3 1/2" x 4 1/2" x 6 1/2" (7.5 cm x 8.75 cm x 11.25 cm x 16.25 cm), but encourage children to experiment with strips of their own to make the pinwheel design. Help children measure and cut out two yellow pieces and two green pieces. Glue the pieces to a 9" x 9" (22.5 cm x 22.5 cm) pink quilt patch as shown in the diagram.

Glyph Factor

Directions for making glyphs are found on page. Ask the children which kinds of ice-cream cones they prefer. Have the children record their answers on their ice-cream patches.

◆ If students prefer cake cones, use blue quilt patches.
◆ If students prefer sugar cones, use pink quilt patches.
◆ If students prefer waffle cones, use white quilt patches.

Fruit-and-Nut Patch

Some flavors of ice cream are made with a delicious array of fruits and nuts. Brainstorm a list of ice-cream flavors made with fruits and nuts. Write the fruits and nuts on the chalkboard. For example, strawberry, cherry, banana, walnut, pralines, peanuts, pistachios, and so on. Invite children to choose a fruit or nut shape to cut or tear from construction paper. Have children glue their favorite fruits and nuts on light blue 9" x 9" (22.5 cm x 22.5 cm) construction-paper patches.

Ice-Cream Cone Patch

Pass out scraps of burlap and instruct children to cut out ice-cream cone shapes. Then ask them to cut out scoop shapes from felt. Encourage children to glue the pieces to a 9" x 9" (22.5 cm x 22.5 cm) yellow patch. Have children glue on chocolate chips cut from brown construction paper or draw on sprinkles.

Literature Connections

Book Activity

Read the book *Frog and Toad, All Year,* by Arnold Lobel (HarperCollins, 1976). Share the chapter about ice cream, and laugh over the antics and miscalculations of the characters. Another "delicious" read is *Jamberry,* by Bruce Degen (HarperCollins, 1995). Read the book several times for children to become familiar with the rhythm and rhyme. Invite the class to recite it as a choral reading.

Pocket Chart

Review this familiar ice-cream rhyme by writing it on sentence strips to place in your pocket chart.

I scream, you scream,
We all scream for ice cream.

Brainstorm with children other food rhymes, writing each new rhyme on a sentence strip. Here are some rhymes to get you started: hop and soda pop; skip and potato chip; cry and apple pie.

Hanging Poem Chart

Encourage the class to help you write a class poem, using each student's name and the favorite ice-cream flavors. Write the following rhyme on your hanging chart, putting in your own name and favorite ice-cream flavor, too.

Choclate chip ice cream is a treat.
It is fun for Mrs. Jones to eat.

Go around the room and have children tell you their favorite kinds of ice cream. Write new verses by filling in each child's name and favorite ice-cream flavor. Invite children to draw pictures of their favorite ice-cream flavors. Cut out the pictures and glue them to the hanging chart.

Class Book—Cone Concoctions

Everyone knows that ice cream can come in cones. But what other fabulous things might an ice-cream cone carry? Encourage children to think about something wonderful they'd like to receive in an ice-cream cone—for example, books, stuffed animals, or baseballs. Pass out drawing paper and ask children to draw their cones filled with fun treats. Make sure children also write a caption for the picture, such as, "Nori likes cones filled with new sneakers." Select several students to make a cover and write a title, "Our Dream Cones," then staple all the pages together. Read the book with your class to see everyone's cone concoctions.

Ice-Cream ABCs

Challenge children to come up with an ice-cream flavor for each letter of the alphabet. Assign a letter to each child. Then instruct students to draw the flavor and write an alphabet sentence about it, such as, "A is for almond fudge." Or, "B is for banana ripple." If children can't think of a flavor, challenge them to make one up. Have students share their ice-cream flavors with the class. Combine all the pages into a class book, or display children's drawings on a bulletin board titled, "Ice Cream From A to Z."

Writing Journal

When do children like to eat ice-cream? Encourage them to recall specific times, such as on a warm summer night, at the swimming pool, or at the park. Ask the children to write about the best times to eat ice cream in their writing journals. Have children draw pictures to illustrate their experiences, too.

Math Activities

Graphing

Create a bar graph on chart paper, and elicit from children different ice-cream flavors. List the flavors down the left side of the graph. Then ask children, out of all the flavors listed, which are their favorites. Point to a flavor and ask the children to raise their hands to cast their votes. For each vote, draw an ice-cream cone. Interpret the graph with the class. Which ice cream is the most popular? How can children tell?

Estimation

Hold up a carton of ice cream and ask children to estimate how many scoops they think the carton contains. Write their ideas on the chalkboard. Then scoop ice cream into separate small paper bowls as children help you count. Whose estimate was correct? Pass out the bowls of ice cream for children to eat.

Patterning

Invite children to use colored dot stickers to create stacks of scooped ice cream. Suggest that they arrange the dots in a vertical pattern, such as ABAB, then draw ice-cream cones underneath with a brown marker. Encourage children to share their patterns during circle time, challenging their classmates to read and recognize the patterns.

Measuring

On an 8" x 11" (20 cm x 27.5 cm) sheet of oaktag, create a template of a large ice-cream scoop. Have each student trace the scoop onto construction paper, then cut it out. Encourage children to work in groups to use all the scoops to measure items around the room. For example, children could lay the scoops across the floor to measure how wide and long the room is. They could tape the scoops to the wall to see how tall a door or bookcase is—or even measure you! Make sure students record their measurements—for example, "The length of the classroom is 35 scoops." Have the groups compare their measurements.

Money Matters

What do children need to buy ice cream? Money, of course! Draw an ice-cream menu to place in your math center, along with pennies or play money. Set a spending limit, for example, 10 cents. Then have children count out pennies to figure out how much an ice-cream sundae will cost. Here are some ideas for your menu.

scoop of ice-cream	5 pennies
hot fudge, strawberry, or butterscotch topping	2 pennies
nuts	2 pennies
whipped cream	3 pennies
sprinkles	1 penny
cherry	1 penny

Science Activities

Research

Bring in a variety of empty ice-cream cartons for children to study. Help children read the ingredients, pointing out that milk is usually the main one. What else do most ice-cream flavors appear to be made with? List their findings on the board. After reading the ingredients, which brand of ice-cream sounds like the one they'd most like to eat?

Sorting

Ice cream is just one of the foods made from milk. Invite children to think of others. Start a two-column chart on poster paper. Bring pictures of foods, and challenge children to sort them into two categories—dairy foods and non-dairy foods. Dairy foods might include milk, cheese, ice cream, butter, yogurt, and sour cream. For non-dairy foods, show children pictures of fruits and vegetables, pasta, rice, and meats. Ask children which dairy foods they've tried.

Health and Nutrition

As you talk about ice cream and other dairy foods with the class, review with children the food pyramid. Explain that nutritionists have devised the food pyramid to help us figure out how much of different foods we should eat each day. The packages of many food products have an illustration of the food pyramid, including cereal boxes, breakfast pastries, and breads. Have children find a food pyramid illustration to bring to class, or have several on hand for children to view in groups. Point out where dairy foods are on the food pyramid, explaining that two to three servings of dairy foods each day is enough. How many dairy products have they had today?

Cooking

Bring a blender to class, along with ice cream and milk. You might also bring in fruit, such as berries or bananas. Then let children help you scoop in ice cream, pour in milk, and drop in berries to whip in your blender for a healthy ice-cream treat.

Research

Did children know that cows actually have four stomachs? Encourage them to see it for themselves by reading *The Milk Makers,* by Gail Gibbons (Aladdin Paperbacks, 1985).

This book provides wonderful illustrations and explanations about how cows make milk. Working in groups, invite children to diagram a cow to show you the four amazing stomachs.

Investigation

This would be a perfect opportunity to visit a dairy farm. Many colleges have agriculture schools, so be sure to check for tours. Explain that you are learning about ice cream, and you would like to see how milk is made. Many dairies even have their own ice-cream shops, and the dairy farmer might make ice cream on the premises for you. Back in class, review with children what they learned. Ask them to write thank-you cards to the dairy illustrated with amazing milk facts they discovered.

Class Visitor—Ice-cream Store Worker

Ask someone in the community who works in a local ice-cream shop to talk about his or her business with the class. Encourage the visitor to tell which are the most popular flavors she or he sells. Also ask your visitor to demonstrate scooping and sundae-making techniques. Afterward, ask children if working in an ice-cream shop is something they'd like to try. Invite children to send thank-you cards decorated with ice-cream cones to the ice-cream shop.

Art Activities

Easel Painting

Invite children to paint self-portraits of themselves eating their favorite ice creams. Suggest that they also paint in details showing where they enjoyed their ice-cream treats. Display the paintings in your school cafeteria.

Bubble Cones

Give to each student a sheet of bubble wrap, then demonstrate how to paint an ice-cream cone right on the wrap, complete with scoops. Before the paint dries, help children press white paper to the bubble wrap, then remove. Have them admire their ice-cream cone prints.

Amazing Animals Quilt

Take a walk on the wild side with this amazing animal quilt. Giraffe prints decorate the border and animal footprints traipse across the patches. See animals roar to life as students create their favorites on quilt patches. This cooperative quilt will be your own class zoo that children can visit again and again.

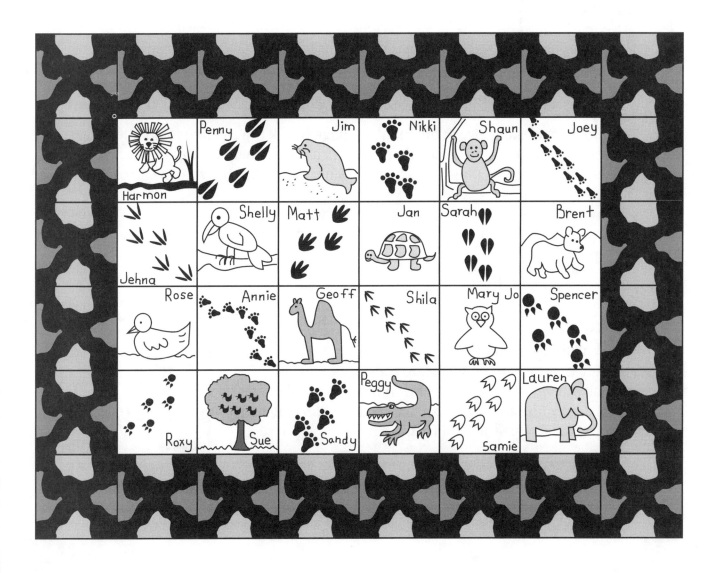

Border Patch

Provide each child with one 9" x 9" (22.5 cm x 22.5 cm) dark brown patch and one 9" x 9" (22.5 cm x 22.5 cm) tan patch. Show children how to draw a free-form shape at each of the four edges of the tan patch, then cut them out. Help children place the shapes at the edges of the dark brown patch, and glue them down.

Animal-Print Patch

Bring wildlife guides for students to flip through to discover animal footprints. Invite children to choose one animal footprint to draw walking across a white 9" x 9" (22.5 cm x 22.5 cm) patch.

Glyph Factor

Directions for making glyphs are found on page 6. Ask the children about their zoo experiences. Have the children record their answers on their animal footprint patches.

- ◆ If students have never been to a zoo, draw tracks walking horizontally across the patch.
- ◆ If students have been to a zoo once, draw tracks walking diagonally across the patch.
- ◆ If students have been to the zoo many times, draw tracks walking vertically across the patch.

Animal Patch

Invite children to create their favorite animals. Supply students with a variety of art materials, including construction paper, crayons, and markers. When satisfied with their animal shapes, provide children with light blue 9" x 9" (22.5 cm x 22.5 cm) quilt patches on which to glue their animals.

Literature Connections

Book Activity

Share the book *Dear Zoo,* by Rod Campbell (Simon & Schuster, 1988). Discuss various animals mentioned in the story. Which animals would children like to see in a zoo? Invite children to write their own letters requesting animals. Have them draw pictures of their animals, too.

Pocket Chart

Copy the following rhyme onto sentence strips to display in your pocket chart.

I saw a <u>monkey</u>
At the zoo.
It looked <u>silly,</u>
Just like you!

Encourage children to come up with other animals and an appropriate characteristic to substitute for the underlined words in the rhyme. For example, lion and ferocious; bear and grumpy; giraffe and tall; penguin and chilly. Invite children to recite the new rhyme with you.

Class Book— "If I Were an Animal . . ."

If children could be any animal in the world, which would they be? Encourage children to draw pictures of the zoo animals along with a caption like, "John would be a lion." Invite student volunteers to create a book cover and write the title, "Zoo Animals." Bind the pages together with yarn. Then send the book home with a different student each night to share with his or her family.

Book Activity and Drama

Introduce the book *Polar Bear, Polar Bear,* by Bill Martin, Jr. (Henry Holt, 1993). Encourage children to create animal masks, drawing the animal faces on paper plates and attaching craft sticks. Have children retell the story as they act it out using their masks.

Writing Journal

Place plastic animals in your "Peek" Box (directions on page 7) for students to view. Which animals do children think they see? Encourage them to choose one of the animals to write about in their journals. Suggest that they draw the animal, then write a few sentences about how this animal makes them feel or facts they might know about it.

Writing Table

Supply your writing table with small blank books. Encourage children to visit the writing table and copy this sentence on each page: "At the zoo I see _____ ." Have children fill in the blank with an animal they might see at the zoo. Then have them illustrate the page with animal rubber stamps or by drawing the animal with crayons or markers.

Math Activities

Graphing

Ask children to name their favorite zoo exhibits. For example, the elephants, the lions and tigers, the polar bears, to name a few. Take a vote of the top four animal exhibits. Write an animal name on the top of each column on a four-column chart. Display the chart in class. During the course of the day, encourage children to visit the chart to sign their names under the exhibits they like best. Share the results in circle time, asking children to explain their choices.

Problem Solving

Invite children to use plastic animals, pictures of animals, or other math manipulatives to figure out simple adding and subtracting problems. Working in pairs, have children begin equations, such as, "Two tigers went to visit four lions at the zoo. How many animals were there in all?" Have children count out the manipulatives to help solve the problem. Encourage them to write the equation, too. (2 tigers + 4 lions = 6 animals.)

Estimation

Show children a box of animal crackers and ask them how many cookies are in the box. Record their estimates on the chalkboard. Then ask children to help you count the cookies. Which student's estimate was closest?

Measuring

Do children know what the largest land animal is? The elephant, of course! An elephant can grow as tall as 11 feet (3.1 meters)! How tall is that? Help children spread out a length of measuring tape, or line up 11 one-foot (30.5 cm) rulers, end to end, along the floor. Have children lay down on the floor, end to end, next to the rulers to see how many children equal the height of one elephant.

"Animal Concentration"

Play "Animal Concentration," (directions on page 6) but with a twist. Children must match animals, but the animals won't be exactly alike. They will be the same kind of animal, but a different species. For example, a grizzly bear and a polar bear. Others you might include are an African elephant and an Indian elephant; an alligator and a croco-dile; a lion and a tiger; a gazelle and an antelope; a seal and a walrus; a gorilla and an orangutan; an iguana and a Komodo dragon; a zebra and a wild horse; a parrot and a toucan. Divide the class into pairs or teams. Have children place the cards face down on the game board. As they turn over two cards, encourage them to discuss with their team member if the animals are similar. If so, the player takes the pair and goes again. If not, it is the next team's turn. The game is over when no cards are left. The team with the most matching pairs wins.

Science Activities

Research

Remind children that a zoo is not a natural habitat. An animal's natural habitat is the place where it is found naturally in the wild. For example, children might see a lion at the zoo, but the lion's natural habitat is the African savanna. Divide the class into groups and help them research the different natural habitats. Assign one of these eight habitats to children to research: a rain forest, the Polar regions, the African savanna, a coral reef, a forest, the wetlands, the ocean, and the desert. Have them explore the library for books on these habitats, then share the books with the class.

Classifying—Animal Families

Invite children to classify animals into the main animal groups of mammals (elephants, bears, people), marsupials (kangaroos, opossums, koalas), reptiles (turtles, snakes, lizards), birds (toucans, ostriches, flamingos), and amphibians (frogs, newts, salamanders). As a class, go through books, both fiction and nonfiction, that feature animals. Point to the animals and ask children if they are mammals, reptiles, and so on. Create a large mural to display on a wall, listing the animal groups across the top. Encourage children to visit the mural to draw pictures of the animals in each group.

Sorting—Animal Habitats

You could also sort animals by their habitats. Divide a bulletin board into eight sections. Ask children to draw pictures of the animals in their habitats on the bulletin board. Here are a few animals for each habitat.

African savanna: lion, elephant, giraffe, zebra
Rain forest: scarlet macaw, ocelot, howler monkeys, toucans
Polar regions: polar bear, penguins, seals, Arctic fox
Forest: bear, raccoon, squirrel, deer
Desert: camel, fennec fox, Gila monster, road runner
Ocean: whales, octopus, tuna, dolphin
Coral reef: clown fish, corals, pufferfish, sea anemone
Wetlands: egret, turtle, crayfish, frogs

Environmental Concerns

Show children pictures of a gorilla, a tiger, a panda, and the scarlet macaw. Challenge children to tell you what they all have in common—they are all endangered animals. Write the words on the chalkboard and ask children to tell you what it means. Confirm that these animals are in danger of becoming extinct. Once the last animal in a species dies, we will never see it again. Explain that environmentalists are always trying to protect endangered animals, but they need our help, too. Invite children to write a class letter to a wildlife organization for information. Here is one you might try: World Wildlife Fund, 1250 Twenty-Fourth Street NW, Washington, DC 20037.

Investigation

A field trip to a zoo is a wonderful way to finish your amazing animals study. Locate one in your area. Try to arrange for a zoo guide to meet your class. As the guide shows children around the zoo, encourage them to notice why each animal is special. Suggest that the zoo guide mention if any of the animals are endangered. Back in class, talk with children about their field trip and invite them to draw pictures of their favorite parts of the zoo. Combine all the pictures into a class "photo" album of your zoo trip. Then have children write a class thank-you note to the zoo.

Art Activities

Easel Painting

Invite children to paint an animal habitat scene. For example, they might paint lions, giraffes, and elephants in the African savanna, scarlet macaws and leopards in the rain forest, egrets and turtles in the wetlands, and so on. Display the paintings around the room to re-create these animal habitats in your class.

Creative Play

Let children set up a zoo in your block area. Suggest that stuffed animals and pictures of animals represent the zoo animals. Encourage them to arrange blocks to form dens and the animals' homes. Then let children guide you, classmates, and other children in school through the class zoo, showing you the animals and sharing information they know about them.

Animal Sculptures

Invite children to mold animals out of clay. When the clay dries, encourage students to paint the models with animal colors. Then display all the clay animals for your own class animal menagerie.